the SACRED WORLD
of the CELTS

AN ILLUSTRATED GUIDE
TO CELTIC SPIRITUALITY
AND MYTHOLOGY

John Duncan's painting, Riders of the Sidhe, *illustrates beings from the Otherworld of Irish mythology.*

the SACRED WORLD

of the CELTS

AN ILLUSTRATED GUIDE TO
CELTIC SPIRITUALITY AND MYTHOLOGY

NIGEL PENNICK

Thorsons
An Imprint of HarperCollinsPublishers

An Imprint of HarperCollins*Publishers*
77–85 Fulham Palace Road
Hammersmith, London W6 8JB

Published in the UK by
THORSONS 1997
1 3 5 7 9 10 8 6 4 2

Designed and produced by
THE BRIDGEWATER BOOK COMPANY LTD

Picture research by *Vanessa Fletcher*

A catalogue record for this book
is available from the British Library.

ISBN 07225 3512 0

Printed in Singapore

Cover illustrations
FRONT: *A ruined early Christian edifice on the Isle of Lewis* (Images)
BACK: (top) *The Headless Green Knight in Arthur's Hall* (The Bridgeman Art
Library/British Library); (bottom): Stonehenge at Winter solstice sunrise
(Fortean Picture Library/Terence Meaden)

A stained-glass window designed by Val Prinsep, from Harden Grange in Yorkshire, depicting Tristan and Isolde receiving the blessing of Isolde's father.

CONTENTS

INTRODUCTION
CELTIC CULTURE

A T THE PRESENT TIME, every aspect of Celtic culture is a very visible part of a multicultural world. Everyone whose family roots lie in central, western and northwestern Europe has a Celtic connection of some sort. Celtic culture is very ancient. It goes back over 2,700 years, yet it is still a living force in the modern world, through Celtic art, Celtic music, Celtic writing, and Celtic spirituality. This is because the civilization of the Celts has continued without break over the centuries. This unbroken tradition can be experienced in the oldest literature from Northern Europe, that is in the Welsh and Irish languages. The earliest Welsh and Irish writings preserve the ancient Celtic world-view that is nature-venerating and poetic, where the spiritual and the material

"The three principal endeavors of a Bard:
One is to learn and collect sciences.
The second is to teach.
And the third is to make peace
and to put an end to all injury;
for to do contrary to these things
is not usual or becoming to a Bard."

T H E   T R I A D S   O F   B R I T A I N

worlds come together to enrich one another. There is also a rich oral culture, with a vast repertoire of story and song that is remembered today.

Throughout history, the Celtic tradition and belief has not remained static, but has continuously developed and progressed in keeping with the times. In ancient days, the early beliefs of the Celts were taken over and reformed by the Druids, who in turn were influenced by Roman religion. In time, this was transformed by Christianity in the form of the Celtic Church, that was not a break with tradition, but a continuation of the Celtic essence in a new form. Although the Celtic Church was finally absorbed by Catholicism, it is a tradition that since the nineteenth century has been growing again in influence.

A romantic, 19th-century portrayal of Stonehenge, in Wiltshire, England — one of the most mystical and impressive megaliths in any Celtic land.

Despite all of these changing historical perspectives, the essence that is distinctively Celtic has maintained itself for over 2,700 years. The peoples known as the Celts are thought to have originated in central Europe, to the east of the Rhine in the areas now part of southern Germany, Austria, Slovakia, the Czech Republic, and Hungary. From around 3,400 years ago, these proto-Celtic peoples expanded across the Continent, and eventually inhabited a large portion of central, western, and northwestern Europe. During the Classical period of Greece and Rome, Celtic culture was predominant to the north of the Alps. Even today, Scotland, Wales, Ireland, Cornwall, Cumbria and Brittany are basically Celtic in character. Despite the changes that time has brought, the influence of Celtic tradition is still fundamental.

Because what we call Celtic culture has existed for more than 2,700 years, and has ranged across much of central and northwestern Europe, it is not easy to define in simple terms. People who need clear definitions of everything find that the Celts are a difficult case. All boundaries are to some extent arbitrary, and depend upon the individual's viewpoint, and so there are several definitions of

A standing stone with traditional Celtic symbols which can be seen at Glencolumbkille, County Donegal in Ireland.

what is Celtic. Ancient writers called the tribes who lived north of the Graeco-Roman civilization Keltoi or Celtae. Others referred to them as Galatae or Galli. All appear to mean "warrior." Some people like to define Celticness through ethnicity. To the Greeks and Romans, they were tall and muscular people, with fair skin, blue eyes, and blond hair tending towards redness. But the ancient Celts seem not to have been a genetically distinct group, and modern Celts do not conform to the Graeco-Roman description. Certainly there were many tribes about which little is known apart from their names and where they lived. What we do know is that each of the old tribes of Europe was distinct from the others, with its own gods, laws, and customs. Even the seemingly strong boundary between the Celtic and Germanic tribes is not so compelling. The founding tribes of the German people − the Cimbri and the Teutones − have Celtic names, while the Brigantes, who occupied southern Britain in the first century BC, were a mixture of Celtic and Germanic peoples.

Subsequently, invasions and migrations have brought the present-day Celts a mixed ancestry. Others see Celticness as language-based. But so many great Celtic writers, from Virgil to Dylan Thomas, have written in non-Celtic languages. Celtic art and music, too, are distinctive, yet difficult to define. Since its inception, Celtic culture has always been able to absorb outside influences and transform them, giving them a distinctively Celtic flavor. All of the Celtic countries, places where, until recently at least, Celtic languages have been predominant, have similar histories. All are on the northwestern fringe of Europe, places where relative isolation from centers of power allowed Celtic culture to remain strong. But politically and militarily, the Celtic countries have not been strong. They have all been conquered by more powerful neighbors, whose governments have often tried to suppress the Celtic languages as a threat to their power. But largely, these attempts failed, and created instead a sense of national solidarity based upon language. The pressures of contemporary mass media and the inter-national power of the English language have proved more damaging to the Celtic languages than direct attempts to wipe them out.

Despite marginalization and political difficulties, Celtic culture has been a major factor in shaping northern European culture. The medieval traditions of chivalry have roots

Hadrian's Wall, which was built in A.D. 122, wends its way across the north of England – an enduring legacy of the Roman incursion into the Celtic world.

A detail from the finely crafted silver Gundestrup cauldron, embossed with the image of a god holding two figures.

in Arthurian Britain and the old Celtic martial arts, while the Grail legends have inspired Christian devotions. Celtic technicians have produced numerous innovations that range from chain mail in pre-Roman times to the steam locomotive trains in the nineteenth century. Celtic spirituality, too, has its own special character within the Northern Tradition of Europe, underpinning the culture and world-view that is especially "Celtic." This book is a celebration of the long history, rich art, and enduring cultural traditions of the Celts.

The stones of New Grange in Ireland are carved with the typically Celtic spiral and lozenge motifs. The division of this stone is believed to mark the solar solstice.

CHAPTER 1

A SHORT HISTORY
OF THE CELTS

THE NAME CELT originated with the ancient Greeks, who called the barbarian peoples of central Europe Keltoi. Rather than being a particular genetic "race," the Celts were a broad cultural-linguistic group. The area where they lived became a constantly changing collection of tribal "nations." The Celts were never an "empire" ruled by one government.

The ancestors of the Celts were the people of the Urnfield culture, so-called because they buried their dead in cremation urns in flat ground. Between 1200 and 700 B.C., they spread westward from their eastern European homeland into the area of modern Austria, Germany, Switzerland, and France. Here, their culture developed into a recognizably Celtic form. The earliest stage of Celtic culture is called the Hallstatt, after a village in the Austrian Salzkammergut where archeologists discovered important artifacts. At Hallstatt and other places with the "hall" (salt) name – Hallein, Halle, Schwäbisch Hall – the Celts' wealth was based upon salt extraction and sale. The technology of iron, too, was embraced by innovative Celtic blacksmiths, who produced the best metal in Europe, that was in great demand outside Celtic areas. An important two-

way trade developed between the Celts and the Greeks, both in their homeland, and their colonies in what is now southern France.

By the seventh century B.C., the Hallstatt people had become prosperous in the salt and iron businesses. In around 650 B.C., the Celts began to rexchange raids with the Greeks and Etruscans, elements of whose culture they

The earliest Celts settled in central Europe
after their ancestors moved there from eastern
Europe. The earliest development of Celtic culture
began at Hallstatt in Austrai.

adopted. By adding and adapting Graeco-Etruscan elements to the Hallstatt culture, the characteristically Celtic style of art came into being. As a result of this, in northeastern France, Switzerland, and the middle Rhine, a new stage of Celtic development took place.

Archeologists call it the early La Tène period, after the definitive artifacts found at La Tène, on Lake Neuchâtel in Switzerland. During the Classical period of Greece and Rome, Celtic culture was predominant north of the Alps. Celtic technicians of the La Tène period were technically superior to their Greek and Roman counterparts. Their superior weaponry, including a new type of sword, chain mail, and chariots, enabled the Celts to mount military expeditions

OPPIDA

The early Celts in central Europe lived in fortified settlements called oppida. *These were large defended villages or towns protected by a defence called the "Gallic Wall"* (murus Gallicus). *This exclusively Celtic structure was made from a framework of horizontally laid timbers filled with stones, faced with a drystone outer wall. Inside the typical* oppidum *were sturdy timber-frame buildings up to 49 feet (15 meters) in length, store-houses, workshops and shrines. The* oppida *were early settlements, and the* murus Gallicus *was made no further west than southern Germany. The techniques of locating and building* oppida *were the foundation of medieval castle-building a millennium and more later.*

against neighboring tribes and nations, including the Greeks and Romans. Celtic fighting men had such a good reputation that they were in great demand as mercenaries. The warrior culture was at the heart of Celtic society, as the heroic sagas of ancient Ireland record.

CELTIC MIGRATIONS

Partly as the result of wars, many Celtic tribes migrated from one region of Europe to another. From their homeland in central Europe, the Celts spread westward into modern France and the British Isles, southwest into Iberia, southward into northern Italy, and eastward through central Europe into the Balkans and Asia Minor. Ancient tribes now thought to be Celtic include the Helvetii, who lived in the area of modern Switzerland, the Boii in modern Italy, the Averni in modern France, the Scordisci in modern Serbia, and the Belgae, who inhabited northern Gaul and southern Britain in immediate pre-Roman times.

However, after the first century B.C., they were in retreat. Driven out of eastern Europe by Slavic tribes, they were vanquished in the west by superior Roman forces. First the Celts in northern Italy came under Roman rule. Then they were overwhelmed in the rest of Gaul (modern France), modern Switzerland, southern Germany, and Austria. Perhaps as the result of the Romans' pressure,

RIGHT: *A medieval manuscript illustrates the legend of the Green Knight, who challenged any of King Arthur's knights to behead him with his ax.*

many of the Belgae emigrated from what is now Belgium to southern Britain in the first century BC. Then, during the first century A.D., most of Britain fell to the Roman conquerors. In the third century A.D., the Celts of southern Germany were overrun by the confeder-

ation of Germanic tribes called the Alamanni. Since then, many centuries have passed, with further inroads into Celtic lands by invaders, yet Celtic culture has never been eliminated from Europe and will no doubt continue to thrive well into the next millennium. Today, Celtic culture is the living heritage of Ireland, Wales, Scotland, Cornwall, the Isle of Man, and Brittany. It has also left its mark on English and French custom and tradition.

BELOW: *King Arthur sustains a mortal wound during his battle with Mordred – a scene depicted in this medieval, illuminated manuscript. Celtic legend tells that Arthur was taken to the Isle of Avalon.*

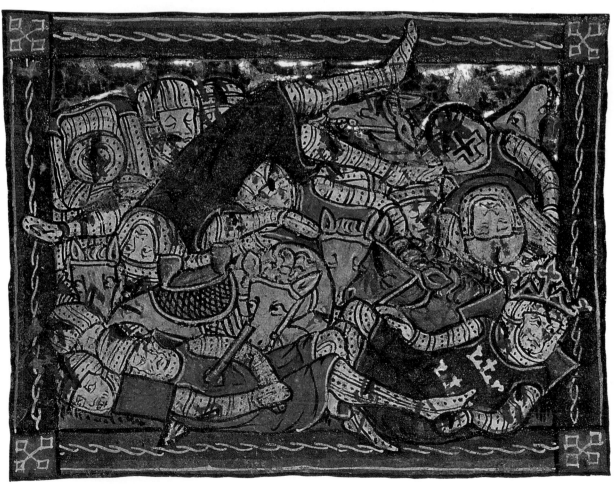

THE ANCIENT BRITONS

The first Celts may have come to Britain as early as the seventh century B.C., and gradually supplanted the indigenous inhabitants. Between 100 and 50 B.C. came a second wave of Celtic settlement, when the Celtic tribes of southeastern Britain came under the control of the Belgae, who migrated from southern Belgium. The Belgae dominated a number of British tribes, that increased in prosperity and material standing, and evolved into politically sophisticated minor kingdoms. The Atrebates and Catuvellauni, which were powerful continental Celtic tribes, also established a foothold in Britain. In 55 and 54 B.C., the Romans under Julius Caesar mounted two military expeditions to Britain. Neither managed to succeed in establishing a permanent Roman presence in Britain, though from then on, certain tribes were pro-Roman.

In A.D. 43, under Claudius, a new Roman invasion was mounted, this time with the intention of conquering Britain. Aided by friendly tribes, the Romans still encountered fierce resistance, but superior organization and training defeated the Celts. In A.D. 61, the Iceni tribe under Queen Boudicca rebelled. After a few successes, she was defeated and killed herself, and the Romans killed 80,000 Celts.

A 2nd- to 3rd-century, northern English, bronze statue of the Celtic smith-god. After the Roman invasion, the smith-god became associated with Vulcan.

The Druids' holy island of Anglesey was sacked. The Roman armies marched northward, and in A.D. 79, entered what is now Scotland. In A.D. 84, the Romans defeated the Caledonians at Mons Graupius, and in A.D. 122, Hadrian's Wall was built from coast to coast to define the northern border of the Empire. Less than twenty years later, the Antonine Wall was built even further north, which marked the northernmost expansion of Roman power into Celtic territory.

THE FALL OF BRITAIN

Between the years 43 and 410, Britain was part of the Roman Empire, during which material culture was transformed. The Celtic tribes north of the wall were never subdued, and remained at a lower level of development. They made occasional inroads into Roman Britain, but

BOUDICCA

Queen of the Iceni tribe, Boudicca led a revolt against the Romans when they seized the part of Britain (now occupied by the counties of Norfolk and Suffolk) that belonged to the Iceni, on the death of her husband, King Prasutagus. After eventual defeat, Boudicca poisoned herself.

were no match for the Roman military. The worst attack came in the year 367, when the Celtic tribal alliance crossed Hadrian's Wall. But at the end of the fourth century and the beginning of the fifth, a succession of important events took place that heralded the decline of Romano-British civilization.

Increased attacks on the Empire in mainland Europe by barbarian tribes led to the withdrawal of Roman forces from Britain to counter these attacks.

The Roman commander-in-chief in Britain, Maximus Clemens, took his forces to Paris to fight the reigning emperor, Gratian. He was defeated and killed in A.D. 388 and thus Britain was left almost defenceless against invading forces. The country was attacked from all sides, by Irish, Pictish, and Germanic raiders. Eventually, after eleven years of chaos, order was restored in Britain by the general Stilicho. But the situation on the Continent continued to deteriorate, as the Roman army proved to be no match for the mighty Goths.

In 401, a significant part of the Roman forces was withdrawn. Successive commanders of the remaining forces staged a series of military coups. In 407 the last of these renegade generals, Constantine III, took the remaining Roman forces across the Channel to stem a planned invasion of Britain by Germanic tribes.

RIGHT: *A French manuscript dating from 1460 illustrates Gawain kneeling at the fountain. One of the knights of the Round Table, Gawain was closely associated with the legend of the Holy Grail.*

Although they defeated the barbarian, the chronicler Procopius wrote: "Constantine was defeated on the battlefield. But the Romans were never able to recover Britain, which from then onwards was ruled by warlords."

letter to the Consul Aetius in A.D. 446, in which they pleaded for the return of Roman forces to fight the invaders. "But in return, they received no assistance." Because there was no help forthcoming, the British king, Vortigern, sent for Saxon mercenaries. Eventually, the Saxons and other Germanic mercenaries rebelled against their Celtic paymasters, and decided that they would take over Britain. However, there was one Briton who, above all others, resisted the would-be conquerors. In the year 497, the chronicler Gildas tells us that Emrys Wledig, who was called Ambrosius Aurelianus in Latin, defeated the Saxons after a fierce battle at Mount Badon. However, it is Arthur, not Emrys Wledig, who is remembered as the Celtic general who halted the westward advance of Germanic settlers.

KING ARTHUR

King Arthur's British victory of Mount Badon stemmed the westward advance of the Germanic invaders for a generation. Except for the conquest of the Isle of Wight by the Jutes, no further British territory was lost. Unlike the other British Celtic kings who fought against the Picts, Scots, Irish, Angles, and Saxons, Arthur is seen as a paragon of Christian virtue. It seems that the Christian religion empowered the British warriors in their desperate fight against the invaders. Later chroniclers saw this time of stalemate as the golden age of Camelot and the Knights of the Round Table.

In A.D. 410, the *Gallic Chronicle* records that Britain was devastated by a powerful Saxon attack. After that, the Britons suffered ever-increasing pressure from the invasive advances of their neighbors. The British authorities sent a

THE BRITISH CELTS
AFTER ARTHUR

After Arthur, the Celts in Britain were disunited. In Strathclyde there was a civil war between British factions. The peasants of Strathclyde (present-day region of Cumbria and southwestern Scotland) were pure Celts, who restored their ancestral beliefs and customs. Opposing them was a Christian faction of noblemen claiming descent from Roman colonists. In 573, these opposing factions fought a battle at Arderyd, near Carlisle, and the Christian Roman faction won.

Four years later, the Saxons of Wessex defeated British forces under kings Ithail and Telpald at the Battle of Deorham. They burned the cities of Bath and Gloucester, and occupied the land up to the River Severn and Bristol Channel. In occupying this land, the Saxons succeeded in cutting the British-held territories in two. Celtic territories in Wales, Lancashire, and Cumbria were cut off from Dumnonia (Dorset, Devon, and Cornwall). The westward pressure continued, until in the year 607, an Anglian army under King Aethelfrith defeated the Celts at the Battle of Chester and broke through British territory to the Irish Sea. Celtic Britain ceased to exist as a unified country.

Following their subjugation by the Romans, Christianity became the dominant religion of the Celts, although the old sacred beliefs never died out.

Now there were three separate Celtic regions, with Anglo-Saxon territory between them. In later years, further conquests saw Dumnonia and Cumbria under Anglo-Saxon rule, leaving Wales as the only remaining part of southern Britain still under Celtic rule.

In 937, the British Celts along with Irish, Danish, and Norwegian allies established a military Confederation. It challenged King Athelstan to fight, not just for his kingdom, but for the very presence of the English in Britain. The Confederation called up a huge army, numbering perhaps 60,000 soldiers. In it were contingents from the Celtic lands of Cornwall, Cumbria, Strathclyde, Scotland, Wales, and Ireland. Its ranks were swelled by an expeditionary force from the Dublin Vikings, reinforced by Norwegian and Danish units.

The Confederation heralds chose the battlefield at Brunanburgh. In Bardic tradition, they marked it out with white hazel posts. Once a battlefield was enhazeled in this way by the heralds, custom decreed that the challenged party must fight on it within two weeks, or lose honor and also the kingdom. Although Athelstan's English army was out-numbered, his warriors fought with enormous courage and won an outright victory.

SCOTLAND

Scotland's Celtic history is as complex as the rest of Britain's. The earliest Celtic inhabitants of what is now called Scotland were a number of tribes, divided broadly into British Celts and Picts. Beginning in the Roman period, the people who came to be known as the Scots migrated from Ireland to a sparsely populated part of northern Britain. According to tradition, Scotland was founded in around the year A.D. 500. A small band of migrants was led by the three sons of Erc, son of Eochaidh: Angus, Fergus, and Loarn. They were of the Race of Conaire, the royal dynasty of Munster in Ireland. The three brothers and their 150 followers founded the kingdom of Dalriada that was named after the Irish region of Dalriada from which they came, and is now part of County Antrim. The family of Angus settled in Islay, while Fergus's followers had Knapdale and Kintyre. The relatives of Loarn occupied northern Argyll. Irish monasteries, too, were founded in western Scotland, most notably St Columba's, set up in 563 on the holy island of Iona. To the north and east of the Scots' settlement were the Picts, who by then had conquered as far north as the Orkneys, and to the south, the Britons.

There were other threats to the Pictish lands. The Angles, who had settled in Northumbria,

RIGHT: *Ferdinand Piloty's idealized, 19th-century, pictorial representation of the court of King Arthur displays a splendid disregard for historical accuracy in terms of his subjects' garb.*

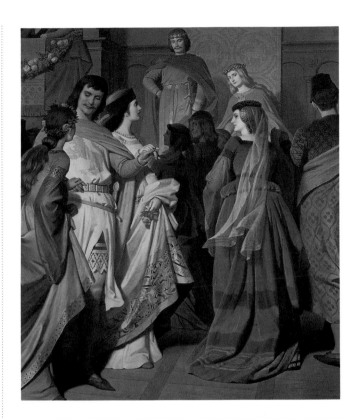

ATHELSTAN, KING of ALL BRITAIN

In around A.D. 930, a British Bard wrote a prophecy called Armes Prydein, which told how the English would soon be expelled from Britain. Flying the Holy Banner of St. David, the Celts would overthrow the rule of King Athelstan. This prophecy was the catalyst for an attempt to destroy the Anglo-Saxon power. However, the prophecy was proved false, the power of the Celts in Britain was broken, and Athelstan assumed the impressive, if inaccurate, title Rex Totius Britanniae, King of All Britain.

GAELIC

Gradually, in the former Pictland, the Pictish language was superseded by Gaelic, the Picts' language was lost, and the Picts assimilated into the new Scottish nation. Until the tenth century A.D., the Scots and Irish spoke the same Gaelic tongue, but afterward they diverged into the two distinct languages that remain today.

attempted to conquer the Picts. It ended with the defeat of King Egfrith's Northumbrian army by the Picts under King Brude Mac Maelchon at the Battle of Nechtansmere in 685. The Picts, who had their own distinctive language and art, became Christian under King Nechtan Mac Derile in the early eighth century. There were also many conflicts between the Picts and the Scots, culminating in a final Scottish victory. In around the year 850, the kingdom of the Picts was unified with that of the Scots under King Kenneth Mac Alpin.

In the early ninth century, Vikings from Scandinavia began their attacks on Scotland, sacking the monastery of Iona and making inroads on the mainland. Finally, the northern and western isles of Scotland were colonized by Norse settlers, and were politically unified with the Norse-ruled Isle of Man as the Kingdom of the Isles. In mainland Scotland, Galloway was settled by the Gallghaideal, a people of mixed Irish-Norse descent, and there were Norwegian

settlements in Caithness and Danish colonies around the Solway Firth. Lowland Scotland increasingly came under English and then Norman influence. King Alexander III, who died in 1286, was the last Scottish monarch of Celtic descent. In 1603, the crowns of Scotland and England were united when the Scottish King James VI became King James I of the

LEFT: The Taking of Excalibur, *by John Duncan, depicts the Lady of the Lake presenting Arthur with her magical sword as a sign that he is the rightful king of England.*

CAMBRIA

The country now called Cymru (Cambria or Wales in English) came into being when the Anglo-Saxons reached the coast of the Irish Sea after winning the Battle of Chester in 607. From then onward, the territory of the Britons was divided into three. In the north, Cumbria, the land of the *Gwyr y Gogledd* (The Men of the North) was later settled by the Norse. Eventually, in the thirteenth century the Cumbrian language died out. To the south, the Britons were forced back from Somerset and Dorset into Dumnonia, the modern Devon and Cornwall, until finally only Cornwall remained as an independent Celtic kingdom. That, too, succumbed to English expansion when it was conquered by King Athelstan in the tenth century. However, Cornish was spoken as an everyday language until the eighteenth century. Unlike Cumbrian and Cornish, Welsh is a living Celtic language, spoken today.

The central Britons, however, were not so readily defeated. Cambria was divided into a number of kingdoms, the most powerful of which were Gwynedd, Powys, Dyfed, and Glywysing, that existed already in the sixth century. In Dyfed at that period, there was Irish settlement, and for a time, the rulers of the kingdom were Irish, while the kings of

new union. London, not Edinburgh, became capital of the new United Kingdom. England and Scotland were unified by an Act of Parliament in 1707. In 1715 and 1745, many highland clans rallied round and supported the Jacobite rebellions against the British crown, but they were unsuccessful and paid a high price for their rebelliousness.

Brycheiniog were of mixed Irish-Welsh ancestry. In the years 705 and 709, northern welsh forces attacked Mercia, the central English kingdom that bordered Wales. The Mercian response was to build a linear earthwork called Wat's Dyke, that ran from the estuary of the River Dee to the River Morda near Oswestry. Later, between 784 and 796, the border between the English and the Welsh was drawn by the powerful Mercian king, Offa, who had an even bigger linear wall and ditch, known as Offa's Dyke, built along much of the boundary.

With the constant threats from England, there was a tendency toward unification, and smaller kingdoms like Gwent and Ergyng were absorbed early. After the death of King Cyngen of Powys in 854, the kingdom was unified with Gwynedd as a country covering the whole of modern north Wales. In the mid-800s, after the unification of the powerful English kingdoms of Mercia and Wessex, there was an English military campaign in Wales that was supported by the kingdoms of the south. They were resisted successfully by the king of Gwynedd, Rhodri Mawr. But after Hywel's death, the Welsh were divided between the pro-English south, and the independent north. Hywel Dda, Rhodri's grandson, unified the north and south by marrying the king of Dyfed's daughter. He recognized Athelstan as king of all Britain, and after Hywel's death, conflict between the English and the Welsh was no longer a national matter.

Following the Norman conquest of England, they turned their attention to Wales. Hugh, Earl of Chester, invaded Wales in 1079. King Henry II subdued south Wales in 1157. There were significant but unsuccessful uprisings in 1114, 1211, 1245, and again, by Llewlyn ap Gruffudd between 1257 and 1282, after which King Edward I imposed English rule over the whole of Wales. Owain Glendwr fought for independence between 1400 and 1415, but was defeated. The Welsh lord, Henry Tudor, took power in England as King Henry VII in 1485, after killing King Richard III in battle. Wales was united with England by an Act of Parliament in 1536.

BRITTANY

The ancient land of Armorica, now called Breizh or Brittany, was colonized by five Celtic tribes. The territory was conquered by Julius Caesar in 56 B.C., after a fierce sea-battle. Celtic culture was broken in Armorica, and many Celts assumed Roman customs. Rebellions in the years 408, 415–20, and 446 were suppressed, but a more successful one broke out in 447. By the year 453, Armorican units were serving in the army that defeated Attila the Hun in battle at Chälons.

Around this time, British refugees began to settle in Armorica in increasing numbers. The towns that remained were ethnically Armorican, that is, Gallo-Roman, while the countryside became British. The name of the land was changed from Armorica to Lesser

Between 784 and 796, the Mercian King,
Offa, ordered a dyke to be built as a boundary
between England and Wales. Much of it
still remains today.

IRELAND

It is probable that the Celts first entered Ireland in around 300 B.C. This era is recalled in ancient Irish sagas, like *Táin Bó Cualnge*, that tell of a society where independent warriors traveled around the land stealing cattle and pillaging each others' territory. This warrior elite lived in fortified homesteads. They also made artificial islands, called crannogs, on which they lived. Over the years, local clan and tribal chieftains became the clients of regional kings, who themselves were subject to the Ard Righ, the High King. In theory, at least, the High King was supreme sovereign of Ireland, and the gods' representative on Earth.

In the fifth century A.D., St. Patrick brought a change of religion. By converting the High King to Christianity, symbolically, he converted the whole island. In 795, the Vikings attacked Ireland. Gradually, these Norwegian and Danish raids became an invasion. By the year 841, they had founded a settlement at Dublin, and later, Limerick, Waterford, and Wexford. Shortly before the year 1000, the dynasty which had provided the High Kings for 500 years, the Uí Néill, was overthrown by the Munster O'Briens. In 1014, the O'Brien king, Brian Boru, defeated the Northmen at the Battle of Clontarf. The O'Brien dynasty was fraught with internal battles, and finally, they gave way to the last High King, Rory O'Conor. In 1169, the Normans invaded Rory O'Conor's Ireland, and put it under the rule of the crown of England.

Britain, to distinguish this British land from Great Britain. Gradually, the Armorican town-dwellers integrated with the British immigrants, and a Breton identity came into being.

After the barbarian conquest of Gaul, the Frankish kings viewed the Breton monarchs as clients. In 507, the Franks captured Nantes, but Brittany remained independent. After 511, when the Frankish king Clovis died, the Breton kings recognized the overlordship of the Franks. Nomeno revolted and regained independence in 841. Brittany was conquered by the Northmen in 921 and subsequently, Brittany was taken over by France.

LIFESTYLE AND SOCIETY

T HE CELTS DID NOT HAVE a caste society, though there were well-defined classes. At the top was the noble class. At some periods of Celtic history, the top man was a king. Often, the king was the head man of an individual tribe, though in later times, nations composed of several tribes came under royal rule. In its most refined form, kingship was seen as divine – rulers were men through whom the gods spoke. Kingship was not necessarily inherited, for kings could nominate their successor. The law of royal succession among the Picts was through the mother, though invariably the monarch was male, and often the king's father was a foreigner. There were also queens, who sometimes ruled in their own right. Among them are the legendary Irish warrior queen, Maeve, and the British Boudicca, who led the rebellious Iceni against Roman rule in A.D. 61.

LEFT: *Lancelot courts King Arthur's beautiful queen, Guinevere, in this richly decorated 15th-century French illuminated manuscript. Many legends relate to the lovers.*

But kingship was not the only form of rule. In Gaul, before the Roman conquest, kingship was abolished by several tribes, including the Aedui, Lexovii, Lemovices, Santones, Remi, and Treviri. Instead of a king, a magistrate, the *Vergobret*, elected by the nobility, headed the tribe. The real power was in the hands of the noble class, whose status came from hereditary right. Noble lineages contained men of honorable origin, linked to other families through marriage alliances. They owned the land, and from their ranks came the military generals and the Druids. In Wales, this class, the *cenedl*, ruled until the Norman conquest.

However, in Celtic society there was not a rigid class system imposed by birth. The landless commoners had the possibility of personal advancement by making a fortune through commerce or war. Some of the lower orders who had fallen upon hard times became clients, having pledged themselves to serve a powerful nobleman. But such an obligation was different from slavery, and the commoner did not give up his rights. Caesar wrote that the object of clientage was to ensure that all common people should have protection against powerful people. Each nobleman had to guarantee that no harm should come to his supporters. If it did, he lost face, and fell in status. Clientage was a form of social welfare, with obligations on both sides. The nobleman supported the client with gifts, that required repayment by loyal service. Unlike some societies, where slavery was hereditary, and there was no chance of future generations becoming free, the Celts' slaves were captive foreigners without civil rights. They could always be freed, to become the client of the noble who had freed them.

Slaves could not fight in times of war. Other men had the right to bear arms, but not all, for some were only permitted to fight when their lives were threatened. In Gaul, it was only possible to go to war if the common people and the priesthood consented, having received favorable omens. Although there was always a commander-in-chief, wars were conducted by an assembly called the Armed Council, that had the final say on strategic matters. Several times during the Gallic War that Caesar won, the Gaulish commander, Vercengetorix, had to give account of his conduct of the war to the Armed Council.

Harp-playing Bards both entertained and informed their listeners with stories and songs, for there was no written tradition of early Celtic lore.

THE BARDS

The Bards knew their songs and poems by heart, and nothing was written down. The instruments of bardism – the voice, the pipes, and stringed instruments – transmit their knowledge by means of sound. Just as there was no written record of saga and song, so there was no musical notation.

THE BARDIC TRADITION

The Roman author Strabo wrote that among the Gauls there were three groups of men who were held in exceptional honor: the Bards, the Vates, and the Druids. The Bards were the musicians, singers, and poets. The Vates were soothsayers, diviners, and natural philosophers. Ancient Celtic religion, that underpinned every aspect of everyday life, was nature-venerating and polytheistic, recognizing many levels of supernatural beings and divinities, female as well as male. The Celts believed that the course of nature is the will of the Gods. Thus they venerated both local and general deities, usually in natural sanctuaries, especially shrines at springs, rivers, lakes, and in woodland. The Bards, Vates, and Druids had an integrated relationship with the natural world. They possessed an immense body of traditional lore, concerning nature, the seasons, astronomy, life, death, and transformation. Most of the ancient skills and wisdom of these men are known still, underlying contemporary Celtic spirituality, that is the synthesis of past and present that is essential for a continuing, living tradition.

The Celts have always held the arts in the highest regard, especially the spoken word. The highest honors were reserved for the Bards, and the Druids taught their students a highly developed art of memory. The ancient Celtic world-view took nothing literally: everything was expressed through poetic metaphors that accessed the invisible inner nature of things that cannot be put into words directly. To the ancient Celts, sound was the primary means of disseminating wisdom.

In former times, the gold or silver branch was the symbol of the Bards. In Irish and Manx myth, the god-messenger Manannan bears a silver apple branch. This was the magic wand of the fairies, with silver bells upon it. It created a special sound, the Music of the Silver Branch, that took the hearer to the otherworld through sleep induced by its elfin music. In the *Agallamh an dá Shuadh* (*The Dialogue of the Two Sages*), "Neidhe made his journey with a silver branch over him. The Anradh, or poets of the second order, carried a silver branch, but the Ollamh, or chief poets, carried a branch of gold; all other poets bore a branch of gold." That this had a physical reality in former times was proven when an actual artificial branch, complete with gilded leaves, was discovered at Manching in Bavaria. In tenth-century south Wales, at the court of Hywel Dda, the Bards were all honored members of the court. Pre-eminent was the *penkerd*, "chief singer," who sat next to the *edling*, the king's appointed heir. Second came the *bard teulu*, the Bard of the Royal Entourage, who owned untaxed land and a horse given by the king, and a harp and gold ring by the queen.

Even under foreign rule, the Celts never lost their literary tradition. In north Italy, under Roman rule, Celtic families produced many outstanding men of letters in the Latin

Celtic crosses incorporate the solar wheel, a symbol of the Celtic sun-god, into the Christian cross. This 10th-century example, flanked by a round tower, is at Monasterboice in Ireland.

language, among them Cato, Catullus, Varro, and Virgil. In later centuries, in northern Europe, the sagas and songs of Irish, British, and Breton Bards were the basis of western European literature.

THE DRUIDS

According to Julius Caesar, in Celtic Gaul there were only two classes of men who had any importance – the Druids and the aristocrats. The common people were treated little better than slaves. They could do nothing on their own initiative, and they played no part in public affairs. The Druids were the Celtic priests and judges. They had a hierarchical organization that was headed by an arch priest who was

BELOW: Ancient British Druids presided over festivals during which the sun was worshiped and honored with animal sacrifices. The snake, whose image appears here, was a symbol of regeneration and fertility.

succeeded on his death by the next senior in rank. If there were two or more potential successors of equal rank when the time came to choose a new leader, then the new archdruid was elected. As priests, Druids were exempt from military service and were not subject to the same level of taxation as the common people. The high status of Druids attracted a continuous stream of candidates, who had to undergo a rigorous training. Although they used Greek writing for their everyday business records and accounts, the spiritual part of the Druidic learning was oral, and students had to memorize tens of thousands of verses, a process that could take up to twenty years. According

to contemporary accounts, the Druidic philosophy originated in Britain, and spread across the Channel to Gaul. In Caesar's time (55 B.C.), Druidic students went to Britain to complete their higher education. According to contemporary accounts, Druidic teachings concerned the nature of the totality of existence, including cosmology, astronomy, physics, and theology. The Druids were the priests who supervised public and private sacrifices and gave judgments on religious questions. They were held in great respect as judges and dispensers of justice, both at the personal and the inter-tribal level. Sometimes, they were called upon to arbitrate in time of war and made the opponents stop when they were about to form up their battle lines. They judged all criminal cases, including murder and interpersonal disputes over boundaries of land or inheritance. They passed sentence and awarded damages. If anyone refused to accept the Druids' judgment, they were immediately excommunicated, being excluded from attending public sacrifices. The excommunicated person lost his or her civic rights, being shunned by everybody because of ritual uncleanness. An annual synod of leading Druids was held at a sanctuary near Chartres, the place counted as the central point of Gaul.

Henry Rowlands' 18th-century depiction of a wise old Druid bearing an oak branch. The oak was sacred to the Druids and represented masculine strength.

Apart from being a general council that discussed religious and organizational matters, the synod was also the supreme court. Litigants from all over the country came to Chartres each year for final judgment upon their legal cases.

CELTIC LAWS

The early forms of Celtic traditional government were based upon oral law, and so little is known directly. However, there are many indicators from several other sources. There are some general principles of Celtic law, that promote the welfare of the whole of society. Caesar tells us that in Gaul, on marriage, a husband added an equal amount of his own property to his wife's dowry. This money was kept as a joint account,

DRUIDIC TEACHINGS

Central to Druidic teaching was the doctrine of the immortality of the soul and its reincarnation. This was thought to be a good incentive for courage among warriors, because belief in immortality made men fearless of death. As well as the indestructibility of the human soul, the Druids taught that the universe was also indestructible, although both fire and water would at some time or another prevail over them.

and the profits were treated as a pension fund, being saved until either the husband or wife died. Then the money and any profits added to it became the legacy of the survivor. Because law should exist for the benefit of all of society, the old Irish laws had provision for hospitals, where orphans, weak, ill, and old people could be cared for free of charge.

As with everything Celtic, legendary history names the founders of law. In Britain, the Molmutine Laws were codified by King Dunwallo Molmutius. The sacred status of roads, still called "The Queen's Highway" in Britain is originally from

"The three gains that will turn out
a loss in the end:
To gain fame for an injurious feat or act;
To gain wealth by injustice;
And to gain mastery in evil contention."

THE TRIADS OF BRITAIN

Molmutius. In Ireland, Brehon Law was founded by Ollamh Fodhla. Irish Brehon Law, named for a judge, Breitheamh, has been called the oldest surviving law system in Europe. The Welsh laws as we know them were formalized by Hywel Dda, the south Welsh king, who called together represen-tatives from all over his realm to standardize the traditional laws that existed in earlier law books. In these texts, all of the legal terms are Celtic, with no trace of Latin influence. From this it is clear that the laws had survived from earlier times without being Romanized.

Hywel's laws deal with such issues as the right of a king to nominate his heir, the *edling*, and other rights and obligations. The Welsh penal code was set out in a detailed and precise manner. It laid down the penalties for murder, insult, or injury short of murder, and theft. The code also ordered the payment of exact sums in compensation for specific injuries, such as the loss of a limb, or the rank of the slain individual. Property was valued in great detail, including such individual items as the royal barn, swords with golden hilts, gameboards, harps, and livestock, including bees and cats. There are no surviving ancient Cumbrian or

GALANAS

A wrong done to one member of the kindred was counted as a wrong against all, creating a "blood feud." By the time the laws were written down in Wales, blood feuds had been replaced by the payment of galanas, "blood money." But the right of vengeance was still reserved if blood money was not paid. Blood feuding continued among the clans of Scotland until the eighteenth century, and sectarian conflict in Northern Ireland has a similar character today.

Scottish law codes, but parts of the later Laws of King David have traces that parallel Irish and Welsh law. Like them, fines were paid in cattle. The Brehon laws continued to be used in parts of Ireland until the seventeenth century, when they were superseded by the laws of the United Kingdom.

THE VATES

The ancient Celts experienced the world as a magical place. Everyday life was lived in direct contact with unseen powers: their world was bound up intimately with the world of the gods. The ancient Celts knew that events in the world were meaningful. Significant dreams were remembered and interpreted. Also, all manner of hidden things could be learned from nature. They could obtain knowledge of the future from observing the flight of birds and the behavior of certain animals. The reading and interpretation of these omens was the duty of the Vates, a special class of diviners. Although less famous than the Bards and the Druids, they were essential members of Celtic society. Unlike the Bards and Druids, who had a formal education lasting many years, the Vates operated differently. Ability was the only qualification for a Vatis. This could come as the result of a revelation, through illness, or by having undergone an ordeal, either accidentally or voluntarily.

ABOVE: *An image from a 14th-century French illuminated manuscript depicts Josephus, the son of Joseph of Arimathea, celebrating mass; the central feature is the Holy Grail, from which the figure of Christ emerges.*

Celtic divination took many forms. The Vates watched the flight of birds, the behavior of animals, and the patterns of flowing water, the tides, and the clouds. They cast stones or specially carved sticks and observed the patterns that they made. From these omens, they were able to guide the Druids and lords in their decisions.

CLAN TRADITIONS

Everything in Celtic tradition has a mythological basis, and many Celtic clans claim descent from their totemic beasts. These animals are recalled by the names of gods, the most widespread of which were Tarvos, the bull; Mullo, the

The English Battersea Shield, dates from the 1st century B.C. The swastika motif was a solar symbol.

donkey; Moccos, god of swine; Epona, the horse-goddess; Artio, goddess of bears, and the cattle-goddess, Damona. According to Julius Caesar, the ancient Britons revered animals such as hares, chickens, and geese, which were never killed. Some Gallic personal names were animal-based, such as Brannogenos (son of the raven) and Artogenos (son of the bear), and the name of one of the most famous of ancient Celts, King Arthur, means "the bear."

The martial arts of ancient Europe, both Celtic and Germanic, had perfected styles of fighting based upon animals. A bear-warrior would fight in the manner of a bear, and so on. These techniques were the basis of the skills of the medieval knights, who often had heraldic animal emblems on their shields. Today, many Scottish clans have animals as their emblems. Campbell of Breadalbane, MacIver, and MacKinnon have a boar as their sign, while Campbell of Cawdor and Lindsay use the swan. The emblem of Clan Bruce is a lion. Clan Chattan, MacGowan, and Mackintosh have a cat; Colquhoun, Davidson, Forbes, Fraser of Lovat, Keith, and Scott, a stag; MacLeod, a bull, and Kennedy, a dolphin. The clans also have their own distinctive woven patterns and colors, the oldest of these have symbolic meanings.

SUPPRESSION

Although the Christian church absorbed much Druidic lore, divination was frowned upon, and the function of the Vates was suppressed. St. Columba condemned the various means of divination then in everyday use in the Celtic folk-tradition, including omens, portents, and the use of the wooden lots or crannachar, on which the characters of ogham were inscribed:

"Our fate depends not on sneezing
Nor on a bird perched on a twig
I adore not the calls of birds...
Nor lots in this world."

CHIEFTAINS
AND PRIESTS

The tribe, clan, or family in traditional Celtic society had two leaders, each of whom held his office hereditarily. The first was the warlord or king, who was supreme commander in both peace and war. Subordinate to the supreme commander, but no less important, was the Druid priest. He was the religious counterpart of the warlord or king. Below the king was the secular ruling class, the aristocracy. Similarly subordinate to the chief priest were the lower priests, or the religious members of the clan. Thus, there were two parallel hierarchies in Celtic society, a secular one and a religious one. The members of the religious group served the secular group by performing public and private religious ceremonies. In turn, the secular group supported

BELOW: *A raven appears to the Irish hero, Fionn mac Cumhaill. Ravens or crows were symbols of death and destruction, but also of prophecy.*

the religious one financially through tithes and concessions, and physically by defending it. This was the structure during pagan times, when the aristocratic group paralleled the Druidic one.

When the Christian religion superseded paganism, the relationship of the people to the land did not change. Traditional tribal and clan territories were maintained: animal husbandry, agriculture, various techniques of hunting, transportation, the skills of craftsmen and women, the martial arts, and the punishment of crime were conducted as before. Human sacrifice, where it still occurred, was banned by the church. Christian priests and monks took over the social position that the Druids of the sacred group had occupied formerly. Druids did not have to pay taxes, and were supported by tithes from the secular community, and this continued under Christianity. Druids were not allowed to carry weapons, but were defended against attack, and this tradition was applied later to the Christian monks and priests.

LEFT: *Harry Clarke's illustration,* Étain, Helen, Maeve and Fand, Golden Deirdre's Tender Hand. *These strong women were all celebrated as Celtic heroines in Irish legend.*

Most of the social functions of the Druids were taken over by Christian priests, and, just as pagan Celtic priesthood was hereditary, so it remained once Christianity was the official religion. All over the Celtic realms, newly converted Christian monks and priests took the

The Irish tradition in particular venerated war goddesses, rather than gods, as their tribal protectors, a role which the mortal Boudicca also assumed.

same career path as their Druidic ancestors. Thus, Christian priests continued all of the Druidic functions, but reinterpreted them according to the new Christian doctrines. The sons of priestly families, who would have become Druids, instead became Christian priests. As holy places were the ancestral property of the families that provided the priests, the new Christian priests inherited them from their pagan forebears. The former pagan holy places were re-consecrated, and monasteries or churches erected there alongside

CHRISTIAN BARDS

As the nineteenth-century Welsh Bard, the reverend J. Williams ab Ithel, noted in 1862 in Barddas: *"The Bards believed that all things were tending to perfection; when, therefore, they embraced Christianity, they must on their own principles have viewed it as a stage in advance of their former creed."*

the holy trees or standing stones, that were Christianized by having a cross cut upon them.

The first Christian priest who practiced at any holy place was usually buried there when he died. He thereby joined his pagan ancestors who were also buried there. The Christian priests were remembered as the saints who had founded the churches, and the places are still called after them today throughout the Celtic lands.

THE CELTIC CLANS

Clann is a Gaelic word that means children. A clan is a family, descended from some notable individual, often bearing his name. The current clan chief, who is the prime descendant of the founder, is nominally the father of the whole clan, having moral authority over all of its members. Although the clan system is Celtic in origin, the contemporary Scottish clans, who have maintained the system in its most ancient form, are of mixed ancestry. Some Scottish clans are descended from the ancient Scots who emigrated eastward from Ireland from the sixth century onward. Others are descended from Norman, English, and Viking notables.

Whatever their ethnic origin, the progenitors of Scottish and Irish tribes and clans are honored today. Some clan founders were Celtic

In Celtic belief, the richly decorated New Grange megalith in Ireland, that dates from around 2500 B.C., was inhabited by the Tuatha dé Danann gods.

monks, others men of royal or noble standing. The diversity of their origins is fascinating. St. Maelrubha or Maree is the patron saint of the Morrisons of Ness, from whom the clan is descended. The Siol Alpin is a group of clans that claim descent from the eighth-century Kenneth MacAlpin, the king who first united the Scots and the Picts in one nation. Conall, fifth king of Dalriada (560–74) was the progenitor of Clan Neill. Clan Gunn is descended from the Norwegian Olaf the Black, King of Man and the Isles, who died in 1237, while MacLeod of Harris is descended from Olaf's brother, Leod Olafson. More generally, the MacPhersons ("son of the parson") are descended from notable Celtic clergy.

The community structure of the clans was formerly universal among the Celts, but this structure was gradually eroded away everywhere except in the highlands of Scotland. Strictly speaking, a clan consists of the chief's family and the branches that can prove descent from the founder through the female line. Although this is the strict familial definition of a clan, it was rarely interpreted so rigidly, and in practice the clan included every family that accepted the authority and protection of the local clan chief. In early times, according to Celtic law, the clan chief was selected from among a specific group of male relatives.

ABOVE: *An illustration from a 14th-century English psalter depicting William the Conqueror hunting. Many Irish clans claim Norman descent.*

However, despite the existence of the chief, in practice the Scottish clan system was a classless society linked by common kinship. The ancestral lands of the clan were shared among the families who farmed them, and were not the sole possession of the chief. But the introduction of the feudal system on Norman lines abolished collective ownership of clan property. The male heir automatically acceded to the title of chief, and the old Celtic system of land-holding was superseded by individual ownership.

The last stand of the highland clans was in support of Bonnie Prince Charlie's claim for the British throne. After the Battle of Culloden in 1746, the British government made a concerted effort to break up the clan system.

Traditional highland costume, including tartan, was prohibited by the "Clothing Act." Old forms of tenancy and agricultural practices were changed, an economy based on money was introduced, and laws were enacted to deprive the chiefs of their customary rights. But the clans were not defeated that easily, and the Scottish clan system flourishes today, though in a modified form appropriate to modern times.

BONNIE PRINCE CHARLIE

Charles Edward Stuart, grandson of James II, was known as Bonnie Prince Charlie. During the Jacobite rebellion of 1745 the Scottish clansmen flocked to support him and he invaded England to claim the throne, but was trounced at the Battle of Culloden the following year.

CHAPTER 3

CELTIC ARTS AND CRAFTS

CELTIC TECHNIQUE was formed through a melding of the Hallstatt culture of central Europe with Greek and Etruscan ideas and methods. From the background of this powerful amalgam, the Celts made striking technical innovations. In central Europe, Celtic technicians improved the quality of life of the people. They introduced the potter's wheel, added iron shoes and wheels to the ancient wooden plow, and invented a simple machine for reaping the harvest. The Celtic carpenters used advanced techniques to make buildings and vehicles. Central European Celtic wagons were superior to any other vehicles of their period. They were built at a technological level that was not surpassed until medieval times. The skill of the wheelwrights was exceptional at the meeting-point of wood- and metal-working. Celtic wheelwrights invented bearings that reduced friction, so that less energy was needed to move chariots and wagons. The ultimate vehicles had roller bearings, that later went out of use in Roman times, and were not used again until the Industrial

This 6th-century dagger and scabbard, beautifully decorated with depictions of animals, is a fine example of the bronze-worker's art.

Revolution. By the tenth century A.D., Irish smiths were capable of making metal strings for harps, and later, during the Industrial Revolution, innovation in iron founding was achieved by Welsh and Scottish technicians.

The metalsmith has always held a high position in Celtic society. Celtic blacksmiths were renowned for their divine inspiration. Celtic smiths invented chain mail, which gave their fighting men a real advantage over their enemies who used bronze armor. The Celtic steel sword was the direct forerunner of the knightly sword of medieval Europe. Analysis of metal found in Hungary shows that the Celtic smiths knew how to make iron and steel containing different proportions of carbon appropriate for each metal's use. Metal was such a valuable commodity that the ancient Britons used iron bars as a form of currency.

RIGHT: *Horned figures decorate this bronze vessel, dating from the 8th century B.C. Vessels such as these symbolized rebirth and were often buried with the dead.*

CELTIC COINS

Most Celtic tribes had their own mint. Celtic coins were made by placing rounded, cast blanks of precious metal on a fixed lower die, into which the upper die was hammered. The great skill of the coin die-cutters reflects a general high ability of goldsmithing, with sophisticated granulation and filigree techniques apparent in many surviving artifacts.

The bronze-workers' skill was no less stunning than the blacksmiths'. They used sophisticated casting techniques to make exquisite tools, jewelry, and armor. As opposed to later art, where a snobbish division was drawn between "fine arts" and "crafts", Celtic tradition knows no distinction between ornament and utility. Unlike some art styles, ornament is not just an embellishment of some basic form, but an integral part of it, creating a unique, beautiful utility wherever it is applied.

Even after the Celtic realms came under foreign rule, Celtic technicians continued to develop their innovative skills. Powered transport, upon which the modern world relies today, owes much to Celtic inventors. The Scot James Watt (1736–1819) invented the steam

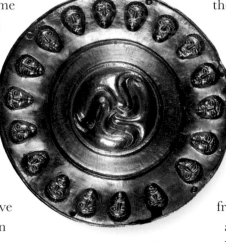

A 2nd- to 1st-century B.C. silver horse harness. Its central triskele and surrounding heads are respectively symbols of the sun and divine wisdom.

engine, and the Cornishman Richard Trevithick (1771–1833) built the first steam-powered railway locomotive, which he ran on the Pen-y-Darran Tramroad in south Wales in 1803. The first successful two-stroke internal combustion engine was made by the Scotsman Sir Dugald Clerk (1854–1932) in 1878, from which came the first motorcycles.

AN INTEGRATED PHILOSOPHY

In both pagan and Christian times, Celtic religion was never separate from the activities of everyday life. The essential Celtic philosophy is that human beings are not separate from nature, but an aspect of it. The things that people make are also part of nature. This integrated world-view means that there can be no distinction between ornament and utility. Nature is beautiful at the same time that it is functional. The patterns and forms of Celtic art are a reflection of the Celtic recognition that the cosmos is composed of ever-changing forms that fade imperceptibly from one form into another, yet always express the same essence. The ancient Bardic teachings of Britain tell how there is an underlying structure of material existence, called Manred. This describes the underlying structure of physical reality: the totality of the particles, atoms, molecules, and geometrical relationships that comprise being. Celtic art is based upon the ever-changing patterns of Manred. The geometrical patterns upon which Celtic tesselations, spirals, and knotwork are based are continuous, without a break. In their plurality, tesselations, spirals and knotwork are interchangeable. They fade into one another. These patterns are fixed artistic representations of the ever-flowing particles of Manred, for all is flux, and the patterns we see at any one time are the patterns of that time, not eternal and unchanging. In Celtic art, the forms of this world and the non-material world interpenetrate one another. In the Celtic worldview, the realms of animals and humans, goddesses and gods, life and death are not separate. They are all aspects of a great integrated continuum, where everything is an aspect of the whole, where the principles of self-similarity reflect the basic way that nature is structured. Each torc, ring, and metal fitment, however small, is a perfect reflection of this principle that integrates the activity of the human world with the natural world.

This bronze fragment was excavated in Italy and depicts a woman dressed in the type of Celtic ceremonial dress that would have been worn in rituals.

The principle of self-similarity at different scales, but precisely related, was reestablished by Benoit Mandelbrot's brilliant discovery of fractal mathematics in 1980. Self-similarity means that patterns are repeated at different levels. There are no empty spaces. Structure is present at every point, reflecting at once both the structure on a smaller and a larger scale. All is an integrated, inseparable part of the whole. This is the guiding principle that has underlain Celtic art since its emergence 2,700 years ago. Self-similarity is integral, manifesting as repeating patterns from the smallest to the largest. There is no place that does not carry the pattern in some way or other. There are no blank spaces, for every part of the cosmos is ensouled.

BENOIT MANDELBROT

A Polish-born American scientist, Benoit Mandelbrot coined the term "fractal geometry" to describe "self-similar" shape, a motif that repeats indefinitely, being smaller each time – a concept associated with chaos theory. Fractals, generated on a computer screen, create models for geographical or biological processes.

SPIRITUAL CRAFTS

To the Celts, making things is not just a material activity, for there is also a spiritual dimension. Recognizing this, people of every trade and profession honored the corresponding god or goddess of their calling. Gallic farmers worshiped Ambactanos, who in Britain was called Amaethon. Gallic wine-growers and beer-makers venerated Sucellos, "the good striker," who protected the vines against all harm. Until the nineteenth century, members of the smiths' Guild of Hammermen took precedence among the tradesmen of Scotland. In Britain, the god Gofannon is the patron of smithcraft. In Ireland, as Goibhniu, he is counted as one of the tre dee Danaan, "the three gods of Danu." In addition to the smith-god, there is Luchtar, god of carpentry, whose practitioners took part in the mystery of the wood. The guilds of differing crafts all had a spiritual basis, with ceremonial initiation ceremonies, grades of competence, and tests of mastery. As a result of these guilds, the Celtic handicrafts were among the best that the world has ever seen.

MANRED

Manred is not fixed, but changing continuously.
As an ancient Gaelic saying tells us:
"With the ebb, With the flow,
As it was, As it is,
As it shall be, With the ebb, With the flow."

The crafts of individual deities were all present in Lugh Ildánach, patron of all arts and crafts, who was known in Gaul as Lugus and as Lleu or Lludd Llaw Ereint in Britain. Irish mythology tells a story about Lugh, the old Celtic god of knowledge and ability. In one

A romantic depiction of Fionn, who inherited his impenetrable shield and sword – symbols of his leadership of the Irish warriors of the Fianna – from his father, Cumhaill.

story, he comes to the court of King Nuada of the Silver Arm in search of employment. The gatekeeper asks him what he can do. Lugh replies that he is a fine carpenter, but he is told that Nuada already has a master carpenter, Luchta, son of Luchad. Then Lugh explains that he is a fine smith, but Nuada already has one. Similarly, when Nuada says that he is a master of the martial arts, a poet, musician, physician, and scientist, he is told that Lugh has all of these, and the best that can be found. But, Lugh asks the doorkeeper, "is there any one in the palace who is accomplished in all of the arts and crafts?" Suddenly it is realized that a man who is a master of all of them is the perfect epitome of human ability, and he is admitted, and given the name Lugh Ildánach, "the all-craftsman." Several cities, ancient centers of craftsmanship, are named after Lugh. In England, London bears his name, in France, the cities of Laon, Léon, and Lyon, and in the Netherlands, Leiden.

A stone head, discovered in Yorkshire, England. The human head was venerated by the Celts, and was therefore a popular motif for craftsmen.

This story shows the Celts' high respect for the person who had gained mastery of his or her chosen craft. Throughout history, the Celts honored those who made the finest craftwork, whether in the material realm, such as metal- and woodwork, or in the sphere of the mind, where poetry, music, and song have always held a high place. Even after the old gods were superseded by the Christian religion, the spiritual principle of Lugh the all-craftsman

could not be abandoned. So he faded from godhood to become Lugh-Chromain, "Little Stooping Lugh," the fairy craftsman. Finally, his name was transmuted into Leprechaun. However, his all-encompassing abilities are remembered in the Irish folksong, "The Dublin Jack of All Trades."

PRECIOUS METALWORKERS

One of the "Three things unprivileged to a Bard, for they are not proper for him," according to Welsh tradition, was "metallurgy, with which he has nothing to do, except to improve it by means of his learning, knowledge, and doctrine." In pagan times, the craft of the smith

SMITHCRAFT

The smith was the most honored of all craftsmen in Celtic society. The trade of smithcraft bordered on the magical, involving the alchemical transformation of dark ore into gleaming metal, and that metal into perfectly fashioned utensils, tools, and weapons. Smithcraft is at the root of human power over the world, for, as an old Irish proverb tells us, "A small axe will fell a large tree."

was a divine art deriving from the otherworldly power of the god Goibhniu or Govanon, who later became the fairy smith, Góbhan Ser. The Celtic precious metalsmiths were true masters of their craft. The Celtic noble, Strabo, tells us: "They wear golden jewelry, torcs round their necks, and circlets on their wrists and arms, whilst people of noble rank wear colored garments sparkling with gold."

Numerous torcs of twisted gold have been found buried in graves and hoards. The largest hoard of torcs ever found came from Snettisham in Norfolk, East Anglia. There were 58 items, dating from around 50 B.C. They include a remarkable piece twisted together from eight rows of entwined rods, and each of these rods comprised eight golden rods twisted together. They are marvelous tributes to the artistry and goldsmithing skills of their makers. Even bronze was inlaid with colored glass enamels in

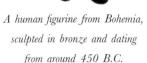

A human figurine from Bohemia, sculpted in bronze and dating from around 450 B.C.

intricate and elegant patterns. From the Romans the later Celtic metalsmiths learnt the skills of making alloys of copper, such as brass, and the technique of plating bronze with silver and gold.

WEAPONS AND HERALDRY

The patterns in Celtic metalwork had a symbolic or magical function. There are many such elements in Celtic weapons. Weapons such as swords and spears had ornament with a magical use. Sword-hilts were in the form of men or gods, and spears were engraved with swirling patterns. Shields, too, bore protective symbols. Surviving ancient shields have animals, such as boars, upon them. According to legend, the Irish hero Fionn Mac Cumhaill carried an impenetrable shield protected by ogham characters in a certain form now called "Fionn's Shield." Other Celtic warriors carried shields with "liuthrindi" patterns that dazzled opponents, an early use of disruptive patterning in warfare. According to tradition, King Arthur's shield bore an image of the Virgin Mary. The complex heraldry of the European age of chivalry may have arisen partly from Celtic motifs.

Celtic heraldic banners showed both the genealogy, geographical location, and fighting style of their owners. MacGorman recounts stories of "dun-coloured standards like fire," and the "streaked satin, black and white" banners of the king of Britain. Telling of another conflict, the Bard O'Doherty tells us that O'Loughlin's banner at the Battle of Moyragh was "a fair satin sheet" that was emblazoned with "an ancient fruit-bearing oak" and "an anchor blue, with folds of a golden cable." King Arthur is said to have had a standard in the form of a dragon-shaped windsock.

An exquisitely crafted, 8th-century, silver-gilt reliquary from Lombardy. Although Christian figures dominate its decoration, it also displays the intertwined vegetative motifs that are typical of Celtic art.

art of *idearmanachd*, in which they read omens from running water, both by means of its visible patterns, and from the sound it made.

This interconnectedness of all Celtic culture appears in the most unexpected places, such as the board game called Brannumh or Fidcheall. This ancient rival of chess was more than just a pleasant pastime, for both its board and the arrangement of the playing pieces on it were symbolic of the order of the kingdom. A poem written by the medieval Irish Bard Tadhg Dall O hUiginn describes Tara, the seat of the High King, as the

INTERCONNECTIONS

All Celtic culture is interconnected, both with art forms in other media, and the forms of the natural world. This is because Celtic culture does not separate itself from nature, but learns from it and enhances it. It is said that the ancient Bards could understand the language of the birds and the trees. Certainly nature has always been a prime inspiration for Celtic artists of all kinds, as the ever-flowing patterns of nature provide endless inspiration. Sometimes, harmony with nature brought inspiration and otherworldly knowledge. The Vates read omens from the flight of birds, the shapes of clouds, and the direction of the wind. After the professional Vates were abolished, the Irishwomen known as Banfathi conducted the

CELTIC HERALDRY

The Irish Bard, Finn MacGorman, who died in 1160, left a poem about the Battle of Magh Rath that describes the banners carried by the units that fought there.

"Great symbol of plunder floating from its staff,
Is over the head of Congal advancing
A yellow lion towards us.
The insignia of the Craebh Ruadh
Such as the noble Conchobar bore
Is now held up by Congal..."

central point on the game board of Ireland: "The centre of the Plain of Fál is Tara's castle, a delightful hill, out in the very middle of the plain, like a mark on a multi-colored Brannumh board. Go forward there, it will be a profitable step. Jump on to that square, proper for the king. Fittingly, the board is yours." The gameboard thus represented the land, and vice-versa. The game's name in Welsh, Tawlbwrdd, means "wood-wisdom," a poetic metaphor meaning "The Game of the Wise." In ancient Wales, judges carried a Tawlbwrdd board as a sign of office, symbolizing law and order through-out the land.

This intimate connection between the small and the large appears again and again in Celtic artifacts.

A pair of brightly colored Celtic horse brasses. Each color had symbolic significance to the Celts.

In the burial discovered at Hochdorf near Stuttgart, a great bronze cauldron was unearthed, which contained a finely worked golden dish. This showed the typically Celtic principle of self-similarity, where the form of smaller, inner objects reflects larger, outer ones. The inner vessel at Hochdorf was duplicated by the larger cauldron that contained it. In turn, the cauldron itself lay beneath the similarly shaped earth mound, and that, in turn, was below the bowl-shaped sky. Similar principles underlay the geometry of manuscript art, such as that found in *The Book of Kells* and *The Book of Durrow*, which contain exquisite illuminations. It appears also in the symbol of Celtic Christianity, the Celtic Cross, that reflects the multiple forms of the sunwheel, the cosmic axis, and the cross of Christ.

COLOR IN CELTIC ART

✿

The colors used in traditional Celtic art were made from natural materials and each of them was symbolic. The Celtic tree-alphabet, Ogham, ascribed each letter to a specific tree. But each character also represented a color, so the artist could hide messages in color within his or her art. Although we see plain stone when we look at a Celtic Cross today, when they were made, every part of them was painted with vibrant colors.

TARTAN

The patterned cloth called tartan is one of the most characteristic of all Celtic folk products. Although only a few ancient fragments have been found, there is no doubt that it is of great antiquity. Fragments of tartan have been found preserved in peat bogs. Roman writers tell us that the ancient Celts wore excellently woven cloth patterned with variegated colors, and a medieval Irish bardic legend puts the date of tartan as far back as 939 B.C. According to this legendary history, the 26th king of Ireland, Tigernmas, introduced the wearing of variegated colors. The number of colors in the cloth that a person wore was an indication of the social status of the wearer. The higher the person's rank, the more colors that were allowed in the tartan.

The Highland cloth called *breacan* is a kind of woolen weave that is woven in stripes of various colors crossing at right angles to make a regular pattern. Originally, it was woven from the long wool of the Highland sheep, a breed now extinct. The weave used for tartan is called "twill," where the

BELOW: *The bright colors of this depiction of Edward the Confessor are features of Celtic art.*

threads first cross over two, then under two, making the effect of a diagonal rib on the web. The proportion of different colors used in a tartan is called the *sett*. Most tartans are symmetrical, the sett being the same for both directions in the weft and warp of the cloth. Similar techniques were used for the traditional cloths of Ireland and Wales. Wherever it was made, Celtic cloth was colored with lichens, bark, and other vegetable dyes that had a mellow quality lost when modern chemical dyes were introduced. Dark, natural colors are the most appropriate for huntsmen and warriors to use as camouflage. In Scotland, where the patterns were most developed, the pattern of a tartan was specific to the place where it was made. A person's home village or island could thus be identified by the tartan he or she wore. A similar principle exists around the coasts of the British Isles in the colorful and variegated knitted patterns of woolen garments such as jerseys and ganseys.

Cumming's painting, The Duchess of Gordon Raising the Gordon Highlanders, *illustrates the clan affiliations proclaimed by the Scottish tartan.*

THE UILLEAN PIPES

The most highly developed bagpipes in the world are the Irish Uillean Pipes, that have the melodic range of the oboe. Devised at the end of the seventeenth century, the Uillean Pipes are blown by bellows placed under the upper arm. They have ingenious arangements that allow the player to play both melody and chordal accompaniment. There is no other hand-held wind instrument in the world to equal the Uillean Pipes.

In his *Description of the Western Islands of Scotland* (1703), Martin Martin writes: "Every isle differs from each other in their fancy of making Plaids, as to the stripes in breadth and colours. This humour is as different through the main land of the Highlands, insofar that they who have seen those places, are able, at the first view of a man's Plaid, to guess the place of his residence..." Martin told how each weaver recorded the exact pattern of the weave on a *maide dalbh* or sett stick, that had the number and color of every thread upon a piece of wood. In 1830, James Logan told how the weaver recorded the number of threads used in a tartan weave "by means of a small stick, round which the exact number of threads in every bar was shown, a practice in use to this very day."

Historical records of tartan go back to the late Middle Ages. In 1488, the Scottish lord, Stewart of Garth, had a war-plaid, which was dark green on one side, and red on the other. Red was the symbolic color of war, and it was worn reversed in time of peace. King James V of Scotland wore tartan when hunting in the Highlands in 1538, and King Charles II wore tartan ribbons at his wedding in 1662. In 1689, a Bardic chronicler told of the tartans worn by participants in a military campaign. Macneill's plaid had all the colors of the rainbow, Maclean of Duart was in plaids with bright yellow stripes, and Glengarry's forces were wearing tartan woven in triple stripes.

BAGPIPES

Although the bagpipe has a long history and wide range throughout Europe and western Asia, today, the instrument is most associated with the music of Celtic nations. This is because the bagpipe has reached its peak of development in Scotland and Ireland. In

The natural motifs in Celtic art, as seen in this horse brass, illustrate the Celts' belief that the human and natural world were inseparable.

former times, Irish and Scottish warriors fought their battles to the accompaniment of drum and war bagpipes, and other, less martial bagpipes accompanied song and dance. According to folk-tradition, the bagpipes have an otherworldly origin. Once, a piper of the Macrimmon clan visited the Piper's Cave at Harlosh Point on the island of Skye. There, the Queen of the Fairies gave him The Silver Chanter of the Fairy Woman, with which he founded the pipers' school of

The Piper's Cave at Harlosh Point on the Isle of Skye, where a piper was given The Silver Chamter of The Fairy Woman.

Borreraig. Pipers trained there served as personal pipers to the clan chief, the MacLeod of MacLeod. Another ancestral clan pipe, The Black Chanter of Clan Chattan, was given to a MacPherson piper by his lover, a fairy woman.

Although it has died out in Wales and the Isle of Man, it is still an important instrument in Brittany, Ireland, and Scotland. In Brittany, the folk bagpipe is called the *biniou*. It is a mouth-blown bagpipe with a single drone pipe. It is traditional to play the *biniou* in a duet with a player of the *bombarde*, a penetrating reed instrument that plays an octave below the bagpipe, the theme of the *biniou* echoing the lead of the *bombarde*. The Scottish bagpipes are the best known and most widely traveled of all Celtic instruments. Originally, the *piob mhor* of Scottish clansmen in the Highlands was a fearsome instrument used in war. It is the loudest of all bagpipes, being blown directly by the mouth. Like the Breton pipes, it has pipes that drone, but instead of the single pipe of the *biniou*, it has three. The earliest part of a bagpipe of this kind is preserved in Edinburgh, and dated 1409. The *piob mhor* was developed

Not only is this horse brass decorated with motifs drawn from the natural world, but its shape is reminiscent of flower petals.

by the addition of further drones, until the present powerful arrangement of three drones was reached.

In the time of Queen Victoria, the Highland Bagpipes were introduced to the British Army, and used in the stirring pipe-and-drum bands of Scottish regiments. They remain an important element of British military pageantry. Today this Celtic bagpipe appears among the military bands of the Palestinians, Iraqis, and it is also played as far afield as the Indian sub-continent.

Early in the twentieth century, attempts were made to reconstruct the old Irish "war pipes"

RIGHT: *A bronze head protects a bucket, believed to date from the 1st century B.C., that was excavated in Aylesbury, Kent.*

ti debet ab hostio recedere n longitudi
nem brachu sui cu uige usus ianitorem.

exquo rex intrauerit aulam donec oinf

ABOVE: *One of these characters depicted in a medieval manuscript wields a leafy branch – each tree had sacred significance in Celtic belief.*

according to an account in Derrick's *Image of Ireland* (1581). The re-constructed Irish war pipe was made by removing one of the drone pipes from the Scottish Highland pipes, and retuning the chanter. This reconstructed Irish war pipe has gone out of fashion.

PIPING THE TROOPS

The ancient Celtic warrior spirit manifested in the tradition of using the bagpipes in war was continued in World War II. On June 6th, 1944, under enemy fire, Bill Millan, personal piper to Lord Lovat, led invading Scottish troops ashore on the D-Day landings in Normandy, playing his Highland bagpipes in war according to ancient tradition.

CHAPTER 4

CELTIC MYTHOLOGY AND FOLKLORE

"Time is a good storyteller"
IRISH PROVERB

THERE ARE NO EARLY written records of Celtic legend and myth. The only direct knowledge we have comes from artifacts that can be understood from later written material. We are fortunate to have many rich objects from burials at Hochdorf, Vix, and elsewhere. We also have artifacts such as the Gundestrup Cauldron and the Coligny Calendar, sacred images of goddesses and gods, and memorials of the dead. Although the myths were written down centuries after the first flowing of Celtic civilization, they reflect every aspect of ancient Celtic life. But there are some significant gaps, such as the complete absence of a Celtic creation myth and an end-of-the-world scenario. Despite these omissions, Celtic myths are a treasure house of traditional ways of thinking, the ethics, laws, and traditions of earlier times.

LEFT: *The Men-an-Tol stones near Morvah in Cornwall. The holed stone symbolizes the goddess, the upright stone the god.*

Although there is no specific creation myth, Celtic legend tells how the first human beings were trees that were transformed by divine powers. In his *Aenid*, the Romano-Celtic writer Virgil tells how the woods "were first the seat of sylvan powers, of nymphs and fauns, and savage men who took their birth from trunks of trees and stubborn oaks." The

TREE CULT

Specifically Celtic lore asserts that the first woman was a rowan tree and the first man an alder. In Celtic literature, the Bardic tradition is often described in terms of trees, wood, and carpentry. The medieval Welsh Bard Iolo Goch (1315-1402), wrote:

"I will bear for Owain
In metrical words, fresh and slow,
Continually, not the hewing of Alder wood,
By the chief carpenter of song."

poetic references to trees do not solely apply to the Ogham alphabet, where each letter is related to a tree. In the Welsh language, many words for awareness, knowledge, and writing include the element of the word, *wydd*, "wood." These include *arwydd*, a sign; *cyfarwydd*, information; *cywydd*, a revelation; *gwyddon*, a wise man; and *derwydd*, a Druid. Bardic poetry often uses wood terms as metaphors for poetry, speech, and learning, calling Bards "carpenters of song." In the sixth century, the "Primary Bard" Taliesin wrote:

> *"I am the fund of song,*
> *I am a reader,*
> *I love the branches and the tight wattles."*

A thousand years later, in 1530, the Welsh Bard Harri ap Rhys Gwilym wrote:

> *"The degrees and roll of wood-knowledge,*
> *The roots of sciences, for the weaving*
> *of a song of praise."*

The trees, from which men and women were born, also provided the inspiration and materials for Celtic poetry.

In general, Celtic tales are archetypal. Druids, saints, and wizards employ magic, foretell the future, and discover hidden things. Kings and warriors embody the noble qualities of justice and honor, while the Bards talk with the birds and bring insight. There is always a

RIGHT: *In Celtic belief, these stones in Rock Close, in the grounds of Blarney Castle in Ireland, possessed magical powers.*

recognition that this world is not the only level of existence. The otherworld of spirits, gods, goddesses, demons, and ghosts is always very close to the surface of reality, acting upon it in all sorts of ways. Celtic tales develop in a symbolic manner that describes the general consequences of particular actions. They are not arbitrary fiction, since they contain thousands of years of human experience whose essence is as relevant today as it ever was.

LAND NAMES

The name of the land is an important mythological factor in Celtic culture, and, as with all things in the bardic tradition, one place can have many names, depending upon the legendary or poetic context in which it is being described. The island of Ireland, for example, is known by many names. It is The Isle of the Woods, The Land of Far Boundaries, The Island of Pigs, The Noble Island, and Inis Fail (the island of the Stone of Destiny). It is also referred to by the names of certain national or tribal goddesses: Scotia, Eire, Eriu, F'dla, and Banba. The island of Britain, too, has a series of Celtic names: Merlin's Precinct, The Isle of Honey, and the Island of Prydein. Each name reflects some historic story or myth that goes to make up the bardic description of the place, weaving a dense poetic and mythological tapestry that enriches human life.

NAMING NAMES

There are a number of important principles in Celtic myth, in which the name of anything is paramount. According to Celtic teachings, the true essence of anything is contained magically within its real name. When we know someone's or something's true name, then we have power over it. That is why the real name of the gods was often never spoken, but an epithet or a descriptive name was used in its place. Names like "The Horned One," or "The Good Striker" are not the true names of the gods, but descriptions of what they do. This principle continued when religion became monotheistic, and epithets such as "The Lord" were applied to the Christian God. In the late Middle Ages, the Christian Welsh Bards asserted that: "It is considered presumptuous to utter this name [the name of God] in the hearing of any man in the world. Nevertheless, every thing calls him inwardly by this name – the sea and land, earth and air, all the visibles and invisibles of the world, whether on the earth or in the sky – all the worlds of all the celestials and the terrestrials – every intellectual being and existence..."

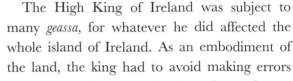

Ancient Celtic society had a system of taboos known by the Irish word *geas*, that were prohibitions and obligations placed on certain individuals. Although they were symbolic, they were nevertheless taken with deadly seriousness. To break a *geas* meant that the transgressor had stepped outside the bounds of society, threatening not only him or herself, but also everyone else. He or she was effectively outlawed, and the punishment was death. *Geassa* included prohibitions on the speaking of certain words or names, the eating of certain foods, abstinence or participation in certain activities, and presence at certain places at specified times. *Geassa* protected holy spirit-places that only divine or sacred persons were considered pure enough to enter, as well as safeguarding sacred objects, and rites.

In a charming combination of figurative and geometrical art, the ingenious design that decorates the North Cross of Ahenny comprises four interlocked female figures.

GWYNN AP NUDD

One of the guardians of the underworld, Gwynn ap Nudd was king of the Welsh fairies and also the Breton god of the beyond. Both he and Gwythyr ap Greidawl contended for the hand of Creiddelad every May Eve until doomsday, as a result of which Creiddelad was fated never to marry. Gwynn ap Nudd's holy hill was Glastonbury Tor.

The High King of Ireland was subject to many *geassa*, for whatever he did affected the whole island of Ireland. As an embodiment of the land, the king had to avoid making errors that would then be reflected throughout the whole country. So long as he conducted himself according to the correct sacred rules, the land was governed properly, in conformity with transcendent principles, and all was well. By performing the proper rites, saying the right words, and observing the *geassa*, the beings of the otherworld would not be offended, and no punishment would descend on king or country. It was an awesome responsibility.

THE KINGDOM OF FAERY

The Celts have a rich folklore concerning the spirits of the landscape. Each class of spirit is well described and understood. Although tales of the Irish leprechaun and banshee have been told all over the world, we can encounter many other earth-spirits in the Celtic realms. When they are treated respectfully, they will bring prosperity to the farmer and good catches for hunters and fishermen. But if they should be ignored or insulted, they will play tricks on us, or possibly do worse. So, as a mark of respect, food, milk, and water should be put out at night for the little people.

In pre-Christian times, the land-spirits were worshiped as local goddesses and gods. In his *Irish Fairy and Folk Tales*, W. B. Yeats explained that when the pagan gods of Ireland were no longer worshiped and ceased to receive offerings, they grew smaller and smaller in the popular imagination, until they became fairies. Conversely, the pagan heroes of old grew bigger in stature, until they became giants. The guardians of the entrance to the underworld are also old gods who would not disappear under Christianity. In Britain, he is Gwynn ap Nudd, whose holy hill is Glastonbury Tor. In Ireland and the Isle of Man, he is Midir. He guards the entrance to the underworld, preventing demons from swarming upward and invading the Earth.

In Ireland, the Daoine Sidh are either the survivors of an ancient Irish tribe, or fallen angels who are neither good enough for heaven nor bad enough for hell. Their queen is Oonagh, consort of King Fionnbarr. She is a former goddess of the Tuatha Dé Danaan. The little people inhabit ancient earthworks, travel along their own special fairy paths, and sometimes wound humans and cattle with their fairy darts. Like the old gods, they appear most frequently on festal days. They fight at Beltane (May Eve), celebrate at Midsummer, and dance with the ghosts at Lá Samhna (November Eve). In the north of Ireland and Scotland, the gruagach is a helpful spirit who looks after cattle, so long as he treated properly. The leprechaun is strictly the Irish fairy shoemaker,

though the name is used indiscriminately today to describe any Irish fairy-being. The Breton lutin, the Manx phynnoderee, and the Irish cluricaun are household spirits. Although they

Celtic mythology abounds with tales of such Leprechaun-like earth-spirits as those depicted here by Arthur Rackham, who demand respectful treatment from humans in return for their cooperative benevolence.

like to steal food and drink, they keep thieves from the house. Just as house-spirits are attached to a certain locality, so certain places in the countryside have their own sprites. In Brittany, the helpful yann-anôd may appear among the sand dunes on the seashore. In

Ireland, if someone has died violently at a certain place, then their spirit may inhabit the place as the demonic thevshi.

Some Celtic spirits are omens of hard times or death. In Ireland, the supernatural "man of

BANSHEES

Banshees, or the women of the sidhe *as they are also known, often appear in bands of three or nine and are always royally dressed. They appear weeping and lamenting to foretell a death and possess magical powers. Over time they became associated with witches or supernatural beings. Occasionally men would lend the deathless ones of the* sidhe *a hand. Some families are said to have their own banshee, who will let out a deathly wail before one of them dies.*

ABOVE: *George Sheringham's painting,* The Baptism of Dylan, Son of the Wave; *the tale of Dylan Eil Ton is told in the Welsh epic,* The Mabinogion.

hunger," the fear gorta, appeared during times of famine, or actually brought it. In the Isle of Man, he is called the glashten. The Irish banshee is an ancestral spirit who appears as a messenger of death for her family descendants. Each family has its own banshee that dwells close to the ancestral homestead. Another omen of death is the bean nighe, "the washer at the ford," a deathly pale ghost-woman who appears at fords, washing bloodstained clothing. The Breton ankou and the Manx keimach appear in churchyards, and whoever sees one knows immediately that they have been issued with a summons of their own death.

ENTERING THE OTHERWORLD

Celtic legends can be understood on many levels, both as good "fairy tales," as symbolic stories with many hidden meanings, and as teachings of bardic philosophy. An important motif in Celtic legend is the interchange between the world of mortal humans and the spirit world. Useful knowledge and abilities are gained by these exchanges. Often a fairy woman – or a goddess – gives an ordinary man exceptional powers.

There are tales of Irish and Scottish bagpipers bringing back techniques and musical instruments from the fairy kingdom. One typical legend tells of the piper of Dunmore in Galway, who, despite his best efforts, could only play one tune. One night, while crossing a bridge, he played the tune, and

John Duncan's depiction of the gods of the otherworld – the mythical realm in which the Celtic deities live.

an animal spirit, the Púca na Samhna (the Puck of November Eve), attracted by the music, seized him, and put him on his back. Then, he carried him away to a feast at the House of the Banshee, where they asked him to provide music for the evening. He played, and was presented with money and a new set of pipes. Then he was carried back to the bridge, and resumed his journey home. But in his journey to the otherworld, he was completely transformed, because he returned home as the best piper in Ireland.

A similar event is recounted in the medieval Scottish *Ballad of Thomas the Rhymer*, which describes an apparition of the Queen of Elfland to the Bard, Thomas of Ercildoune:

> *"True Thomas lay on Huntlie Bank;*
> *A ferlie he spied with his eye;*
> *And there he saw a ladye bright*
> *Come riding down by the Eildon Tree.*
>
> *Her skirt was of the grass-green silk,*
> *Her mantle of the velvet fine;*
> *At ilka tett of her horse's mane*
> *Hung fifty silver bells and nine.*
>
> *True Thomas pull'd off his cap,*
> *And louted down on his knee:*
> *'Hail to thee, Mary, Queen of Heaven!*
> *For thy peer on earth could never be'.*
>
> *'O no, O no, Thomas', she said,*
> *That name does not belong to me;*
> *I'm but the Queen of fair Elfland,*
> *That I am hither come to visit thee."*

After this introduction, where she denies that she is the Virgin Mary, the Elven queen takes Thomas away to her kingdom. They travel on the otherworldly "third road." This leads neither to the church's destination of reward, Heaven, nor its place of punishment, Hell, but to another pagan place, the Celtic otherworld. Like others who have entered the otherworld while still alive, and come out again, Thomas returned a transformed man, as Thomas Rhymer, a Bard of the greatest skill.

RIGHT: *The* Mabinogion *tells of Rhiannon, the Welsh goddess whose white horse easily outstrode the mount of Pwyll, king of Dyfed.*

The Welsh medical family known as the Physicians of Myddfai received their original instruction from an otherworldly Lady of the Lake, Llyn-y-Van. She gave a bag to the first doctor of the dynasty, Rhiwallon. It contained medicinal herbs, instruments, and recipes. She told him that his mission on Earth was to be a benefactor of mankind by relieving them from pain and misery, and showed him a hidden place where all of the medicinal herbs of the Earth grew. From that, Rhiwallon and his sons became physicians to the local lord, Rhys Greg, who gave them "rank, land, and privileges at Myddfai, for the maintenance in the practice of their art and science, and the healing and benefit of those who should seek their help." Gifts from the otherworld are often abilities, such as the power of healing or the power to sing, or create poetry. However, skills obtained through the otherworld should on no account be used for personal gain, but are there for the benefit of others.

THE BARD TALIESIN

Regarded both as prophet and poet, Taliesin was an early Bard who was drawn into Arthurian legend and is represented as discoursing with Merlin. He became famed for his poetry, and The Book of Taliesin, *possibly compiled during the fourteenth century, may contain some of his authentic writings.*

OTHERWORLDLY TRANSFORMATIONS

The cauldron is symbol of inspiration, plenty, and rebirth. There are two Celtic legends of the cauldron of inspiration, one Irish and one Welsh. In the Welsh legend, Kerridwen's son, Avagddu, was the most ugly and ill-favored man in the world. To counteract this, Kerridwen decided to brew a potion that would make him the wisest man in the world. For magical reasons, it was necessary to boil this brew continuously for a year and a day in Kerridwen's Cauldron of Inspiration and Science. At the end of this period, only three distilled drops of potion would be left. Kerridwen employed the boy Gwion Bach to stir the cauldron, and a blind man Morda to stoke the fire. On the day when the brew was ready, by accident, three drops splashed out during the stirring, and landed on one of Gwion's fingers. He put his finger in his mouth, and immediately gained enlightenment and magical abilities.

Seeing that Kerridwen would destroy him for stealing Avagddu's potion, Gwion fled, and Kerridwen chased him. Empowered by the magic potion, Gwion became a hare, and Kerridwen a greyhound. Then, Gwion jumped into a river and was transformed into a fish. Kerridwen transformed herself into an otter. So Gwion became a song bird and Kerridwen a falcon. Finally, Gwion changed into a wheat-grain, and Kerridwen a black hen who swallowed him. But, having eaten Gwion, she became pregnant with him, and eventually gave birth to him. She had intended to kill the baby, but when he was born, he was so beautiful that she could not bring herself to do it. So she put him in a coracle and set it adrift in the sea. It was washed up in a fish weir, and the baby was saved. When he grew up, the boy became the most inspired of all poets, the Bard Taliesin. Thus, the story of the genesis of the great Bard Taliesin is an enchanting tale of accidental enlightenment, transformation, death, and rebirth.

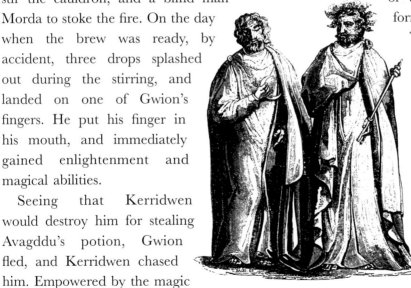

Celtic sacred life was regulated by Druids, Seers, and Bards; the greatest Bard of Welsh mythology was Taliesin.

The story of the Holy Grail is among the most powerful and enduring of all Celtic myths. It is a tale of spiritual hope. In the time of King Arthur, after the fall of Rome, the land of Logres (the Welsh name for England) was devastated through human violence, selfishness, and greed. Then, at a feast, King Arthur's knights of the Round Table saw a vision of the Holy Grail, the cup of regeneration used by Jesus at the Last Supper. They realized that by finding the Holy Grail, they could heal the devastated wasteland of Britain, and restore a just and prosperous land. So the knights set forth on the quest to find it, and many died in the attempt.

The story of the Holy Grail is a perfect amalgamation of pagan and Christian spirituality. The Welsh historian Nennius tells us that at the Battle of Guinnion Fort against the Saxons, King Arthur "carried the image of the Holy Mary, the everlasting Virgin, on his shield, and the heathens were put to flight...through the power of Our Lord Jesus Christ and the power of the Blessed Virgin Mary, his mother." The historical King Arthur's successful resistance against the invading heathen Saxons was a real restoration of the old Roman Christian civilization. The Holy Grail may be no more than an illusion that leads people on a fruitless search to find it. But, though those who seek the Grail may never find the otherworldly vessel in physical form, nevertheless the quest for the Grail will be successful when they find themselves.

OGHAM SCRIPT

Ogham is an archaic alphabet, also called "the Secret Language of the Poets," which played a significant role in bardic teachings. The Ogham alphabet comprises 20 letters, arranged in groups of five, constructed from a series of straight lines incised across a single stave, that were cut along the edge of a stone or a billet of wood.

CELTIC TREE-LORE

An understanding of Celtic tree-lore is important for the interpretation of all areas of Celtic culture. The Druids venerated the native trees of Britain and Ireland. They ascribed different

In its celebration of the natural world, Charles Butler's painting, Willows on the Cam, *evokes the sacred groves of Celtic lore. The Willow is the tree of weaving and binding.*

qualities and virtues to each species, describing their uses both on the physical and magical levels. These were expressed in the many legends and songs that mention trees. In ancient Ireland, the subtle qualities of the trees were formalized into an alphabet of twenty-five characters. This was the mystical tree-alphabet called Ogham, that ever since has been used in divination and magic. The wisdom of the trees became the repository for the ancient skills and wisdom imparted to generations of initiates in the ancient forests and holy groves of Ireland and Britain. This knowledge survives in the folk traditions of most Celtic countries. According to the twentieth-century Irish writer, Dermot MacManus, trees can be classified in the following order of magic power: hawthorn, hazel, elder, willow, alder, ash, holly, birch, oak, broom, and Scots pine.

Willow, used for making baskets and hurdles, symbolizes flexibility and speedy growth. The hazel is the bardic tree of wisdom, promoting fertility, poetry, and knowledge. Peeled hazel sticks were carried by the Celtic heralds, and so long as the white hazel was visible, no fighting was allowed. This is the origin of the white flag of truce or surrender which is used in warfare to this day. Hazel posts were also set up to delineate battlefields, and those challenged to fight were obliged to do so within two weeks, or lose honor. Hazel remains the favored wood for water diviners' rods. The alder is a tree whose wood is especially resistant

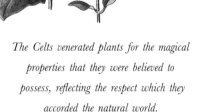

The Celts venerated plants for the magical properties that they were believed to possess, reflecting the respect which they accorded the natural world.

to water, so alder piles were used as the foundations of buildings in waterlogged ground. So, symbolically, the alder is a tree of foundation.

THE BIRCH

The birch is the primary tree of Celtic lore. Symbolizing purification, its twigs make the part of the broom that sweeps away dirt and harmful things. As Beth, birch is the first letter of the Ogham alphabet. It is the customary tree of maypoles. A birch branch on a house is believed to bring good luck. At Christmas, it is traditional to burn a Yule Log of birch wood.

The apple is the Celtic symbol of regeneration and eternal life. It is grown in orchards that, in Celtic law, were specially protected as sacred groves on holy ground. The otherworldly land of Avalon, to which King Arthur was taken after his last battle, means "the place of apples." In Celtic paganism, the oak is sacred to Taranis and Daronwy, gods associated with thunderbolts and lightning. The tree itself is reputed to give protection against lightning, probably because it "courts the flash" itself. Trees struck by lightning, the antler-like "Stag-Headed Oaks," are held in regard as otherworldly trees. In Celtic

countries, it serves as a marker in countryside boundaries, sometimes as a marriage oak, under which couples were married, or a gospel oak, beneath which priests preached. In Wales, the sycamore is a tree of the Bards, in the shade of which fine poetry can be composed. The linden, or lime tree is planted as a central marker, found as the Dorflinde, or Village Tree in Germany and surrounding countries. In medieval times, the linden was the law tree, beneath which judgment was given, and upon which those found guilty were hanged. The Scots pine is a tree of illumination. Resinous slivers of pine were used as lighting in the days before candles, and pine trees were planted as waymarks for travelers at strategic positions in the landscape.

PROTECTIVE TREES

According to Celtic lore, certain trees are protective against various kinds of harm. They are planted next to the door of a house, and their leaves are worn as lucky charms. The hawthorn, or may tree, is one of the most

ROWAN TREE

A rowan tree growing by the garden gate will ward off witchcraft, bad luck, and harmful sprites.
As an old Scottish spell tells us,
"Rowan Tree and red thread
Make the witches lose their speed."

powerful trees. Grown in hedges, hawthorn protects holy ground such as churchyards and cemeteries. Sacred to the god Taranis, hawthorn is said to give protection against lightning. Blackthorn is another thorny hedgerow plant used for walking-sticks and magical staves of Druids, wizards, and witches. It has its own protective spirits. the lunantishee. The bay is the tree of preservation, sacred to the god of healing, Nodens. Planted by the door of a house, it is said to ward off contagious diseases. Bay trees, bedecked with ribbons and grown in tubs, can often be seen outside urban shops and restaurants. In Scotland, Juniper twigs are worn as a charm against the evil eye.

In his *Miscellanies* (1778), Thomas Chatterton recommended "Against foul fiends... the holly bush and churchyard yew are certain antidotes." The yew is the tree of life and death, because, although it is the longest-lived of all European trees, almost every part of it is highly poisonous. The elder is the witches' tree, that has the power to keep lightning away from the house. At Beltane, elder twigs are woven into a garland. Worn around the head, it gives the wearer the "second sight." The ash tree is protective because it symbolizes the principle of stability, being the cosmic tree in the northern European tradition.

LEFT: *A tree towers over one of the stones that form the megalith at Avebury, England, which is believed to date from 2500 B.C., making it possibly the oldest such site in the world.*

THE COSMIC AXIS

The Celts' veneration of trees was a tacit recognition of the cosmic tree as a symbol of the universe and the presence of the other-world. The cosmic tree's roots are in the underworld, its trunk rises through this world, and its branches are in the heavens. At its tip is the Pole Star, around which the heavens appear to turn. The maypole, with its circular garlands, is a physical representation of the cosmic axis. According to late Welsh bardic teachings, existence is divided into four circles of being.

These levels can be viewed as levels of consciousness, and also as worlds inhabited by deities, spirits, and human beings. The cosmic axis that links these different worlds is a channel for spirits, up and down which shamans ride, and gods and heroes journey. Going down the axis into the underworld appears in the Celtic tale, *The Descent Into Annwn*, in which King Arthur visits the nether realm.

The lowest of these realms is Annwn, the underworld. This is "the loveless region," a region generally considered demonic and evil. Above this stands Abred, the material world where we live. In Abred, good and ill exist in roughly equal measure, though good has a greater power than evil. Higher still comes Gwynvyd, the heavenly upperworld, where angelic goodness and light are the ruling principles. Finally, at the very top of the axis is Ceugant, the realm of Hên Ddihenydd, "The Ancient and Unoriginated One," the creator and sustainer of all existence.

CHAPTER 5

CELTIC RELIGION AND SPIRITUALITY

PAGAN CELTIC SPIRITUALITY understood that all of existence has a cyclic nature, and that there is a direct continuity between the material world and the other-world. Druidic teachings, that have come down to us through Welsh tradition, recognized that there is an unseen world that interpenetrates and affects the visible world. Things are not just what they seem. Everything exists on several simultaneous levels. Human beings can understand things as having three levels: the physical, the spiritual, and the symbolic. Thus, Celtic culture was integrated with nature, and expressed itself through the multiple possibilities of life itself. Celtic religion taught the reincarnation of all individual souls, and the appearance of divine beings on Earth.

Recognizing that the whole Earth is ensouled, the pagan Celts venerated many gods, goddesses, and spirits, both local and general. Many gods were venerated throughout the Celtic realms under similar, but different, names. Julius Caesar tells how Dis was the

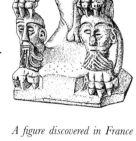

A figure discovered in France depicts a hideous monster resting its paws on human heads.

supreme god of the Gauls. The Druids taught that the Gallic race was descended from this ancestral god, who was lord of the underworld.

The Romans identified Dis with their chief god, Jupiter. Other names given to the Gallic high god are Taranucus (the thunderer), Taranis, and Uxellimus (the highest one). In Ireland, the chief god was the Dagda, whose name means "The Good God," who was also known as Eochaidh Ollathair (All-Father), Ruad Rofhessa (Lord of Great Knowledge), and Aedh (Fire). Teutates is one of the best documented Gallic deities. According to Julius Caesar, the most important god of the Gaulish pantheon was Mercury, that is, Teutates. Teutates was a public deity who protected the people in general. As clans and tribes gradually merged to form larger political units, Teutates became protector of the whole nation.

RIGHT: *A scene from the New Minister Charter (A.D. 966) depicts King Edgar, flanked by the Virgin Mary and St. Peter, commending the charter to the enthroned Christ.*

LEFT: *The Irish goddess Brigit became the Christian St. Brigit (or St. Bride, depicted here by John Duncan), whose feast day is the same date as Brigit's festival, Imbolc.*

The god who was named Belenos in Gaul and Beel in south Germany was one of the most important Celtic deities. In Gaul, Caesar connected him with the Roman solar god, Apollo, as dispenser of light and healing. In Ireland, he was called Bíle, "Father of Gods and Men" and is consort of the mother goddess Dana. In the Welsh *Mabinogion*, Beli Mawr appears as a great ancestral spirit. The Celtic festival of Beltane, May Day, celebrated all over the Celtic lands, is in his honor as the beginning of summertime, that he rules.

Individual tribes were protected by their own goddesses and gods. Some of them were also recognized more widely throughout the Celtic realms. The god Olloudius, whose name means "Great Tree," was venerated in Antibes in the south of France by the Narbonenses. Lenus was an important tribal god worshiped by more than one tribe. God of the Gaulish Treviri, he was also worshiped in Britain under that name, and by the Silures as Ocelos. The god of the Gaulish Allobroges, Vellaunus, was also seen as an aspect of Lenus. Esus, the tribal god of the Essuvii, was worshiped widely in Gaul. The warrior-god Camulos was the tribal god of the Remi. Brigantia, goddess of the Brigantes in central Britain, is known all over Europe under the name of St. Bridget or Brigida, where she is the guardian saint of mountain passes.

BELENOS

❦

Also known as "Sparkling" or the "Shining One," Belenos presides over the feast of Beltane or May Eve, that heralded the release from winter and celebration of summer, although the precise rites associated with him remain shrouded in mystery.

SPECIALIZED GODS

Because warriors were held in great regard, there are several significant Celtic warrior- and battle-gods. Belatucadros and Caturix, "Battle-King," were war-gods worshiped by lower-ranking military men, while Albiorix, "King of the World" was a general war-god. Cocidius was invoked as "God of Soldiers" in northern Britain. Camulos was another important British war-god. It is possible that the name of King

Arthur's castle, Camelot, refers to him. The god Segomo, whose name is an epithet, meaning "Victor" or "Mighty One," was invoked during battle by Irish warriors.

Gods of natural forces were also important in Celtic religion. Leucetius was the lightning-god, Vintius the wind-god, and Vitucadrus, the brilliant in energy. The gods of light and fire were the Gallic Lugus and Belenos. Gods of the ocean, important to a sea-going people, include the Irish Manannan mac Lir, the Welsh Manawydden, and the Scottish god, Shony.

Late Welsh tradition tells of the god Amaethon (Gallic Ambactanos) who was the patron of farming, and Daronwy, the thunder-god, whose name became an epithet of the Christian God in medieval Wales.

Nature deities were also recognized as important by the pagan Celts. There were goddesses and gods of every aspect of nature: rivers and streams, lakes, mountains and

BELOW: *The Castlerigg stone circle, near Keswick in Cumbria, England, stands in a natural amphitheater.*

hills, plants and animals. Some were deities of special localities, while others were general nature divinities. Ialonus Contrebis, the British god of the forest glade, was invoked at Lancaster. The Gaulish god Erriapus is shown on an altar from Saint-Beat as a head emerging from foliage. Perhaps he is the origin of the "green man" that can be seen in medieval churches. The Celtic stag-god in Gaul is usually called Cernunnos. However, the only ancient evidence for the name Cernunnos comes from one incomplete Gallic inscription on a relief

LEFT: *The Irish sea-god, Manannan mac Lir, depicted riding one of his seahorses. He was said to have been the first king of the Isle of Man.*

from Paris. This is of a godly figure with a pair of stag's antlers, and both human and deer's ears. Despite being a rather shadowy figure in antiquity, now this god has assumed importance in modern Celtic paganism.

Water was important in Celtic worship. Goddesses of healing springs, including Sequana, Sirona, and Sulis were revered at therapeutic shrines. Although there are goddess and god names associated with rivers, the holiness of rivers usually came from within and not always from some outer spiritual being that inhabited them. There are six rivers in Britain called Dee, from the Celtic Deva (holy), but Deva was not a goddess, although this is sometimes assumed. Celtic paganism, however, did recognize many water-deities. The greatest of mainland European rivers, the Danube, is holy to the god Danuvius. Father Thames is remembered today in London. Celtic goddesses are also remembered in the names of rivers. The goddess Adsalluta gave her name to the River Savus (Save) in Noricum. In France, Axona is goddess of the Aisne, Sequana of the Seine, Matrona of the Marne, and Ritona of the River Rieu. In Britain, the goddess Clota presides over the Clyde, and Belisama, the Ribble. In Ireland, the river Shannon is associated with Sinend, and the Boyne to Boand or Boann, "She of the White Cattle," and consort of the water-god Nechtan.

THE CELTIC GODDESSES

Pagan religions held the female principle in equal, if not higher, regard than the male. In keeping with this, the Celtic pantheon had many goddesses. The most widespread of these goddesses worshiped in ancient Britain were the Deae Matres, The Mothers, whose Welsh name, *Y Mamau*, is used today for the "little people." They were worshiped especially at certain localities as manifestations of the *anima loci*, when they were given names that reflected their roles as place-guardians. But nevertheless they were recognized as having universal qualities. At York there is an altar dedicated to the mother goddesses of Africa, Italy, and Gaul, while an inscription found at Castlesteads in Scotland reads, "To the Mother Goddesses of All Nations." Another typical dedication is just "To the Universal Mother Goddesses."

The mother goddess had a number of names. She was worshiped as Virodactis in what is now the west of Germany. The specifically Celtic Great Mother was called Ana, Anna, Dana, and similar names. With her consort Beli or Belinus, Ana is the Celtic ancestral goddess. The Welsh royal houses of Dyfed, Gwynedd, and Powys, as well as Saints Beuno, David, and

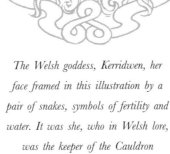

The Welsh goddess, Kerridwen, her face framed in this illustration by a pair of snakes, symbols of fertility and water. It was she, who in Welsh lore, was the keeper of the Cauldron of Inspiration.

GREEN MAN

The Green Man is traditionally clothed in leaves at the May Day festival, that celebrates fertility rites and the regeneration of life. Traces of the Green Man may be found all over Europe, and his face is carved amid foliage on many Gothic churches.

Catwg, traced their ancestry to Anna, who, in Christian terms, was portrayed as the mother, sister, or cousin of Our Lady. Dana was also the mother of the Tuatha Dé Danaan, the generic name for the gods and goddesses of Ireland. Don was her Welsh counterpart. The Irish commentator Cormac (A.D. 831–903) wrote: "Ana is the mother of the gods of Hibernia, well she used to nourish the gods, from whom is said her name *anae*, i.e. abundance ... also Buanann, nurse of the heroes ... as Ana was mother of the gods, so Buanann was mother of the Fiann (the people of Ireland)." Another mother-goddess, specifically the guardian of nursing mothers, was Fuinche. This mother-goddess had three breasts, just like the Christian saint Gwen Teirbron, who took over her role.

There were many Celtic goddesses of love, plenty, and long life. The northern British goddess Setlocenia, "the long-lived one," was a protectress of human life. Fand was "The Pearl of Beauty." Aíne, the Irish goddess of love, was still being venerated in County Londonderry and Tyrone in the nineteenth century. Annona, the goddess of abundant harvest, was shown with a horn of plenty. Rosmerta, the Gaulish goddess of fruitfulness, was depicted with a staff, a serpent, and a money bag.

RIGHT: The White Horse of Uffington was cut into the chalk during the Iron Age. It may have been the sacred emblem of the indigenous Atrebates tribe.

There were heavenly goddesses of light and power. Grian is the Irish sun goddess, revered at Cnoc Gréine at Pailis Gréine in county Limerick. In south Germany the people worshiped the white goddess, Dea Candida Regina, a queen of heaven, who carried an ear of wheat and a scepter. Oonagh, consort of Fionnbarr, is a goddess of the Tuatha Dé Danaan who became the queen of the Irish fairies. Among the lesser spiritual beings, the Celts also venerated female nature-spirits such as the proximae (kinswomen), the oak-sprites called dervonnae, and the water-sprites or niskai.

EPONA

Another important Celtic goddess was Epona, who is often shown on horseback and carrying a basket of fruit that symbolizes fruitfulness. Epona was goddess of the horse, a sacred animal in all northern European traditions, and, as such, she was worshiped widely in mainland Europe and Britain. In France, she had over 300 known shrines.

THE SACRED HEAD

"From the earth, the flesh;
From the water, the blood;
From the air, the breath;
From the calas (hardness), the bones;
From the salt, the feeling;
From the sun, that is, fire, his motion;
From the truth, his understanding;
From the Holy Ghost, that is, God, his soul or life."

THE EIGHT MATERIALS OF MAN,
FROM THE WELSH BARDIC TRADITION

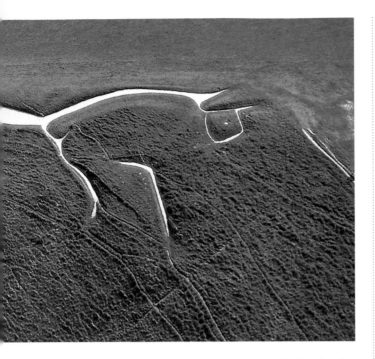

SEVERED HEADS

As a cult object, the head, whether an actual severed human head, or a stone or wooden representation of one, was symbolic of divine powers, providing a link with the ancestral spirits.

Before the Roman conquest of Gaul, the Celts would, as a matter of course, behead the enemies they had killed in combat. Those of high repute were preserved in cedar oil and kept in special boxes. They were brought out on special occasions and shown to visitors. It was a matter of honor that the heads should never be returned to the family or tribe to whom they belonged. According to Celtic belief, the human head contains the essence of an individual's being. The cult of the head was important in Celtic tradition, and it continues today in a limited form in some places. Severed heads of enemies

RIGHT: *A "Celtic" or "Bradford" stone head on the roof of a Yorkshire house. The Celts believed that human heads were symbols of divine power.*

were set on posts at the entrance to forts, and as trophy offerings as at Bredon Hill and Stanwick hill forts in England. The Celto-Ligurian shrine at Roqueperteuse, Bouches-du-Rhône, in southern France, contained skulls set in niches cut in the standing stones at the entrance. Celtic sculptures of monsters holding two severed heads are known from Linsdorf and Noves in France.

In medieval times, other skulls were considered to protect castles magically. In his

preface to Malory's Arthurian masterpiece *Le Morte D'Arthur* (1485), William Caxton notes that Sir Gawain's skull was kept as a relic at Dover Castle. Heads and skulls are also associated with holy wells, and in former times patients seeking a cure would drink from cups made from human skulls, that were never to be removed from their holy places. Even today, superstition dictates that guardian skulls should not be removed from their resting places. In Dorset in western England, Bettiscombe Manor has a human skull that on no account should be taken from the building. When this did happen, the manor was plagued with hideous, supernatural screams that went on day and night until the skull was returned.

The island of Inisgloria, off the Mayo coast, possessed a rack of skulls, one of which was said to be that of St. Brendan the navigator. In former times, fishing boats sailing by would lower their sails in honor of the saint. In churches, too, skulls are venerated as relics in Celtic-influenced places as far apart as Drogheda, Rennes, Toulouse, and Constance. In northern England, in upland areas of the counties of Yorkshire and Derbyshire, Celtic heads are still carved today in some secrecy and set upon new buildings.

CELTIC SACRIFICES

As well as head-hunting, in pre-Roman times the Celts practiced human sacrifice, which was an integral part of religion. They would consecrate a human being as a sacrificial victim, then stab him or her in the back with a sword. The manner of the victim's death throes were interpreted as an oracle. Other Celtic human sacrifice involved shooting them to death with arrows, or impaling them. The most famous Druidical sacrifice was to burn victims in a wickerwork cage in the shape of a human figure. In Gaul, men were hanged on trees sacred to Esus and stabbed. In Ireland, Cromm Cruach, whose name means "blood crescent," had a golden image at Mag Slécht, where people were sacrificed to him at the autumnal festival of Samhain.

Death on the battle-field was treated as a sacrifice. A person going into battle was dedicated to the gods, so that if he died, the gods would receive him.

RIGHT: *A representation of Ogma from Washington, D.C. Ogma was both the Irish Tuatha dé Danann's war-god and the inventor of the Ogham tree-alphabet.*

BENDIGAIDVRÂN

Welsh legend tells of the British king, Bendigaidvrân, who invaded Ireland, and was slain in battle. His followers cut off his head, and brought it back to Britain. Then, for years, they traveled around the country. Each evening, it was set up in a tent, and spoke oracles. Eventually, the head was buried in the holy hill at London called Bryn Gwyn, the White Mount. This is where the White Tower of the Tower of London now stands. So long as the head remained there, Britain was protected from invaders and could not be conquered.

Andraste, "the invincible one," was the goddess of victory of the British Iceni tribe. Boudicca offered up sacrifices to Andraste in a holy grove before fighting the Romans. Another British goddess of death was the slaughter-goddess Agrona, while in Ireland, the goddess of battles and death was The Badb. As Badb Catha, her name means crow or raven, the carrion-loving birds that eat the dead on the battlefield. Herecura or Aericura was a death-goddess who originated on the north coast of the Adriatic, but sacrifices were made to her by the Celts in Romanized south Germany.

Julius Caesar tells us, "Before a battle the Gauls dedicate all their booty to the war god. After victory they sacrifice the captured animals and make a collection of everything else. In many states, on consecrated ground, one can see trophies built up of such material. It is rare that anybody dares to ignore the claims of Heaven and to conceal the spoils of war at home or to steal them from a trophy, for that offence is punished with death by hideous torture."

Animals, usually *geas* (taboo), were sacrificed and eaten at certain sacred festivals. The horse, the sacred animal of Epona, was an important example. After the introduction of Christianity,

St. Columba (521–97) is venerated by Christians for his missionary work in both Ireland and northern Scotland, where he converted the people to Christianity.

the Celts continued to eat horse on their sacred feast days. Pope Gregory III (731–41) condemned Celtic horse-eating as an "unclean and execrable act." In 787, a church council held at Chelsea said that it was a stain on the character of British people. There is still a taboo against eating horseflesh in Britain. But the custom of horse sacrifice was not so easily suppressed. At the monastery of St. Gallen in Switzerland, until the late Middle Ages, horse was eaten in commemoration of the founder, the Irish monk St. Gall.

Even after the introduction of Christianity, the sacrifice of animals was an important part of Celtic religion. In 1589, bullocks were being sacrificed "the half to God and to Beino" in the churchyard at Clynnog Fawr in Wales. In 1678, certain members of the Mackenzie clan were punished by the outraged church authorities at Dingwall for "sacrificing a bull in a heathenish manner in the island of St Ruffus … for the recovering of the health of Cirstaine Mackenzie …"

DEATH AND BURIAL

Julius Caesar remarked that funerals in Gaul were magnificent and expensive events, considering the relatively low standards of life there. Everything that the dead man is known

to have valued, including even animals, went to the grave with him. Not long before his time, Caesar wrote that slaves and retainers known to have been loved by their masters were also sacrificed. Grave goods buried with the dead provided all that a person could need in the otherworld. Because of this, excavations in modern times have enabled the ancient Celts to live again. Burials of noble people excavated in recent times have revealed fine artifacts. They show that the ancient Celts had a profound recognition of the cyclic nature of existence, reincarnation, continuity between the material world and the otherworld.

A mound of earth or a cairn of stones was built over the burial chamber. Sometimes there was a ring of wooden posts around it, and a pole, standing stone, or statue on top of it. These artificial hills of the dead were images of the otherworld. Those who died went inside the mound, leaving the world of the living to reenter the womb of Mother Earth. At death, part of the human spirit passed to the otherworld for regeneration and eventual re-birth. The person's property was taken into the fairy kingdom, and the burial mound became a memorial to the life and deeds of the dead person. It also served as a landmark for travelers and a place of prayer and contemplation. In the British Isles, once burial

RIGHT: *The stag was considered a sacred animal by the Celts, symbolizing fertility, strength, speed, and the divine hunt; it was therefore sometimes a sacrificial creature.*

under mounds had ceased, cairns of stones were built as memorials. They also marked places where a body had been laid when it was being taken for burial in Christian churchyards. It is traditional for passers-by to put a stone on cairns they pass for good luck.

Nothing in a Celtic burial is without symbolic significance. Symbolically, burying

SACRED LAKES

Weapons and treasure captured in war were cast into lakes. Vast treasures lay in Celtic holy lakes. The sacred lake of the Volcae Tectosages at Toulouse, contained precious metal sacrificed to the god Belenos the "Shining One." It was dredged by the Romans, who took away 110,000 pounds of silver and 100,000 pounds of gold.

someone beneath an earth mound is putting them into the otherworldly city, Caer Sidhe. The dead person has left this world and literally entered the underworld. At Hochdorf, near Stuttgart in south Germany, the burial of a nobleman was excavated in the 1980s. It contained a rich array of grave goods, including a whole four-wheeled wagon with an enormous cauldron, drinking horns, weapons, and fine grave clothing for the dead man. Nothing in the burial was arbitrary. Even the clothing of the buried person had symbolic meaning. The dead man's hat was made from birch bark, which is the Celtic hat of the dead.

Wagons and chariots were buried with noblemen and women. They were vehicles to enable the dead person to travel through the otherworld. A number of large vessels have been found in rich Celtic burials. The most notable are the Greek bronze *"krater"* from a noblewoman's mound at Vix in France, and a bronze cauldron from the Hochdorf burial. Celtic mythology has many examples of vessels

THE OTHERWORLD

Seen by Celts as the home of their gods, the Otherworld was cherished as the place of the ever-living. As Loegaire, Cuchulainn's charioteer, entered this hallowed ground he extoled: "At the entrance to the enclosure is a tree/ From whose branches there comes beautiful and harmonious music./ It is a tree of silver, which the sun illuminates./ It glistens like gold."

as a symbol of plenty and rebirth. From later records, we know that the cauldron was sacred to the Welsh goddess Kerridwen and the Irish father-god called The Dagda. Under Christian influence, it became the Holy Grail. Symbolically, the cauldron is the container of wisdom, the entrance to the underworld, and the holder of the healing, regenerative brew that brings the dead back to life.

DRUIDIC COSMOLOGY: THE FIVE ELEMENTS

Druidic cosmology gives a particularly Celtic view of the nature of existence. The best explanation of these teachings is found in *Barddas*, the collection of medieval Welsh texts and more recent commentaries explaining the elements of Druidry and Bardism. It is an entire system, that, in its modern form, is influenced by Christian doctrines. Nevertheless, it has many differences from other European and non-European religious systems, and provides some idea of what the pre-Christian Druids may have believed and taught. One text describes the five elements, thus: "Calas; fluidity; breath; uvel and nwyvre. From calas is every corporeity, namely, the earth and every thing hard; from fluidity are moisture and flux; from breath are every wind, breeze, respiration and air; from uvel are all heat; fire and light; and from nwyvre every life and motion, every spirit, every soul of man, and from its union with the other elements, other living beings." The subtle fifth element, a manifestation of the

LEFT: *Maeve (or Meb), the mythical Irish queen of Connacht, consults a Druid sorcerer in the hope of bringing about the downfall of Cuchulain.*

These took many different forms, each discrete form being but a specialized manifestation of the greater whole. These manifestations are, among other things, described as fairies, leprechauns, sprites, elementals, and dragons. The *Nwyvre* as a semi-abstract power is depicted in the form of the mythological dragon-like being that can be found widely in medieval European art. This beast is shown with the head of a predatory animal, with ears joined to a reptilian body, and one pair of forelegs. Its back bears wings, and its rear part is a prehensile, serpentine body and tail. The Wyvern of English heraldry is the *Nwyvre*. Here, it is distinguished from the very similar dragon by possessing only two legs (the dragon has four). The Wyvern's legs are forelegs, and the posterior portion of the beast is serpent-like. Medieval representations of this symbolic beast are found all over Europe.

divine spirit, was recognized as a reality by the people of pre-scientific, pre-industrial cultures. It is an important element of esoteric teaching, appearing all over the world under many different names. The ancient Greeks talked of the *pneuma*, which the medieval European alchemists identified with the Quintessence, the fifth element. In Celtic lore, it is *Nwyvre*. In modern Welsh, *Nwyf* means energy, *Nwyfriant*, vigor and vivacity, while *Nwyfre* means the sky or "firmament."

The nature of this subtle force is explained in *Barddas*. In keeping with the magical-poetic world-view of the Celts, this subtle force was visualized as non-human yet sentient beings.

BARDDAS

A two-volume work, Barddas *was compiled from materials in his possession by the Welsh Bard and scholar Llewellyn Sion of Glamorgan, toward the end of the sixteenth century, and was subsequently edited and translated by J. A. Williams ap Ithel. An account of considerably philosophic interest, it featured not only Druidic characters and episodes, but also Christian ones.*

THE CELTIC CHURCH

SOUTHERN BRITAIN WAS a province of the Roman Empire, that became officially Christian in the year 313. However, this did not mean that there were mass conversions. In effect, paganism continued in parallel with Christianity, though the funds of the pagan temples were confiscated and given to the church, and Christianity grew in power. Before the Romans withdrew from Britain in around the year 410, Christian missionaries attempted to convert the Celts outside the empire in Ireland and north Britain. In A.D. 397, a British priest, St. Ninian, went north into the land of the Picts to preach Christianity. Ninian built a church at Whithorn in Galloway. A generation later, in A.D. 432, St. Patrick took the Christian religion to the pagan Celts in Ireland. He was successful in establishing Christianity there, and when Britain broke down economically and politically, with internal civil wars and invasions by the Angles, Saxons, and

"The three reasons for worship: to teach wisdom; to cultivate the energies of the mind; and to gladden hope."

WELSH BARDIC

THEOLOGICAL TRIAD NO 46

Jutes, Ireland remained unaffected. Irish society assimilated the Christian religion, and a new, Celtic Church developed in Ireland. Once established, it spread Christianity back into Britain.

Although Roman rule had ended, the British Church retained its links with other Churches. Celtic Christianity included elements of Jewish, Egyptian, Graeco-Roman, and Druidic traditions. As it developed, the Celtic Church adapted the liturgies and theologies of Egyptian, Byzantine, and Frankish Christianity. Just as the Celts of the La Tène era had modified classical art forms, so the Celtic priests took the best philosophical ideas and reworked them into a new, particularly Celtic, spirituality.

CELTIC SAINTS

From the days of the Bards, Vates, and Druids, holy men and women have always played an important role in Celtic society, and there are probably many thousands of individual saints

A ruined early Christian edifice on the Isle of Lewis in the Scottish Outer Hebrides.

*"There are three things from God:
peace, truth, and knowledge; and,
knowing them, it is the duty of all
to communicate them to others."*

THE WELSH BARDIC *TRIAD*

OF ST. PAUL AND BARDISM, NO 5

recognized in Celtic Christianity. Although they are highly respected by all Christians, most of them are not Catholic saints, made by the popes of Rome. Their sanctity comes from popular recognition, and not from official sources. A few of the Celtic saints are known internationally, like St. Patrick and St. Brigid. Others are of national importance, like St. David and St. Columba, while others are

important in their own regions, like St. Teilo and St. Dubricius, who founded many churches in south Wales. Some are associated with specific holy places, like St. Asaph at St. Asaph's in Wales, St. Kevin at Glendalough in Ireland, and St. Kentigern in Glasgow in Scotland. The vast majority of Celtic saints are only of local importance. Many Celtic saints are the subject of myths, folktales, and monkish *Lives*. They range from factual historical accounts at one end to full-blown Celtic myth at the other.

Although these stories praise Christian virtues, they contain many episodes that recall how the Celtic saints continued the archetypal qualities of the older, pagan heroes and gods. Whether these individual saints existed historically or not as individual human beings, the stories of their lives serve as guiding metaphors for a good human relationship with divine powers and nature.

EARLY CHRISTIAN MONASTICISM

*"The three paths towards truth: to understand it;
to love it; and to seek it."*

WELSH BARDIC *THEOLOGICAL TRIAD* NO 33

Christian monasteries originated in the deserts of Syria and Egypt, where some early Christian monks chose to live away from civilization. Living a contemplative life, these early monks sought to come closer to God than they felt was possible in the profane hustle and bustle of the city. They strove to recreate Paradise on Earth, at least internally, by reunifying the body and the spirit, that they believed had become separated. They used spiritual exercises to bring mind, body, and spirit back into alignment. By so doing, they attempted to re-establish the human body as the point of contact between heaven and earth.

The possibility of reunifying human existence with the divine was not to come by rejecting the natural world. The desert fathers did not preach a crusade against the natural world, for nature is the perfect instance of the creative power of God. On one occasion, a visiting philosopher asked St. Anthony how, as a Christian, he could live without a copy of the scriptures. The saint gestured toward the surrounding landscape and answered: "My book, O philosopher, is the nature of created things, and it is present when I want to read the words of God."

Following St. Anthony, other monks also lived without written matter, not even the scriptures, for they saw God's hand in the whole natural world. Celtic Christian intellectuals followed the desert fathers' principles, recognizing that humans are not external to nature. A tenth-century Welsh poem reflects St. Anthony's principle: "The Father has made wonders in this world that it is difficult for us to find an equal number. Letters cannot contain it, letters cannot express it." This deeply profound understanding that spirituality exists within nature is one of the most significant elements of Celtic religion.

The change from paganism to Christianity did not come as a complete revolutionary break, but rather as a transition. Of course, Christian philosophical interpretations replaced pagan ones, and the totality of nature was

RIGHT: *An angel exhorted Caedmon (d. 680?), an illiterate herdsman, to compose narrative religious verse, whereupon he retired to an English monastery in order to comply.*

PARADISE ON EARTH

✤

St. Paul of Thebes (died c. A.D. 341) and St. Anthony of Egypt (died A.D. 356) believed that the fall of man was not irrevocable. They taught that through spiritual excercises, the natural state of grace could be restored. Once this disharmony was resolved, they believed, spirit and matter would come once more into alignment, and human beings would regain their state of harmony as the likeness of God in harmony with all creation. Their task was to end the unnatural separation between the physical and the spiritual world, at which point the Kingdom of God would be present in the material world as well as in the spiritual realm.

LEFT: *In a profoundly religious moment typical of the mystical communion with God experienced by many early Celtic Christians, the devout Ethne hears her name called out.*

viewed not as existing in its own right, but as the handiwork of God. But Celtic Christianity still recognized the existence of an unseen world interpenetrating the visible world. It retained a particular reverence for the world of nature and its spiritual forces, that it perceived as revealing the presence of the divine.

CELTIC CHRISTIAN ASCETICISM

"Three things which a man ought to avoid, as he would the fall of fire on his heart: pride, cruelty, and covetousness; for where they are, all his doings will degenerate into ungodliness, irreligion and all mischievousness."

WELSH BARDIC *THEOLOGICAL TRIAD* NO 54

The spiritual exercises and techniques of the desert fathers were very harsh on the body and mind. To the Celts, this way of living was called "white martyrdom," contrasted with the "red martyrdom" of being killed in witness of belief. Unlike many Christian martyrs, the vast majority of Celtic pioneers and missionaries were not killed for their beliefs. In Britain and Ireland, where Druidism was the

RIGHT: *An image from an early Christian manuscript, illustrating the 7th-century St. Cuthbert making a sea voyage in order to spread the Christian gospel.*

predominant pre-Christian religion, there were very few instances of martyrdom. Trying to emulate their eastern role models, the early Celtic monks traveled to "deserts," uncultivated, wild places that lay far from human presence. The names of several Irish monasteries, like Dysert O'Dea, recall this tradition. However, despite their attempts to emulate the desert fathers, the Celtic monks inhabited quite different "desert."

The northern "deserts" were completely unlike hot, arid deserts of Asia Minor and North Africa. They were cold and wet rather than hot and dry, and were alive with wild animals and birds, many of them very dangerous to human beings. Vegetation was also rampant rather than sparse. So, although the monastic intention was the same, there arose an important difference between the Mediterranean tradition, where Christianity came into being, and the Northern tradition. In the hot regions, arid deserts threaten to overwhelm and dry up civilization. But in northern Europe, untamed and lively, wild nature threatens to enter and overwhelm the fragile world of human beings.

The dangers of the northern "deserts" were thus quite different in character to the sandy wastes of the south. To survive in the dry desert, the monk needed passive resistance. But in the north, he needed to take active measures against dynamic natural forces that could kill him. The nearest that the Celtic monks could get to the terrain loved by St. Anthony and his followers were rocky places. They favored especially the vigorous environments of islands or places right next to the sea. In this way, wild rocky islands such as Caldey, Priestholm, Scelig Mhichil, and Iona became important Celtic monastic centers.

THE MARKS
OF THE PRIEST

The theological traditions of the Celtic Church came from several different spiritual sources. But as individuals, the founding fathers of the Celtic Church came from a Druidic background. So it was natural that they should adapt Druidic concepts and merge them with Christian teachings. St. Patrick said "Christ is my Druid," and the learned St. Columbanus was called "The Prince of Druids." In addition to the native Druid tradition, there were elements of Coptic Christianity from Egypt. Like the Celtic Church, the Coptic one had also arisen in a pagan milieu, and adopted some of the customs and traditions of ancient Egyptian religion. In this way, a unique form of native spiritual Christianity was created. Many of the early Celtic churchmen actually came from Druidic families, having been educated in the traditions of Celtic paganism. Because of this, the Celtic Church conserved many of the ancient myths and customs. A tonsure or shaven head has been the identifying characteristic of a priest from ancient times, and it was adopted by early Christian monks. The ritual baldness of the priests of Isis and Serapis had been established for 300 years when Christianity was introduced to Egypt, so St. Jerome advised that Christian monks should not shave their heads lest they be mistaken for pagan priests. Despite St. Jerome's warning, the tonsure was not abandoned as the mark of a Christian monk. The eastern Church copied

ASCETICISM

Many Celtic spiritual exercises were very physical. Lives of Celtic saints tell how they would fast and pray all night, up to their neck in the water of a holy well, or in the sea. The medieval Welsh Bard, Lewys Morganwg, tells us how St. Illtyd worshiped:

"The fasting and penance of his faith
Would he, bare-headed, daily undergo;
And each night, in a cold spring,
Would he remain naked for a whole hour."

Like their Egyptian forebears, the Celtic saints sought hardship as a means to resist the temptations of the world.

TATTOOING

In pagan times, many Celtic tribes tattooed their bodies with emblems to acknowledge the pagan gods. Because of its pagan meaning, tattooing was banned in Britain in the time of St. Kentigern, and so it never became associated with Christian priesthood, as it did in the Byzantine Empire, where Christians were tattooed with crosses.

the Egyptian tradition of shaving the whole head. This is known as the Greek Tonsure, or the Tonsure of St. Paul. The western Church shaved the head differently, in the Roman Tonsure, or the Tonsure of St. Peter. This is the familiar Catholic monk's tonsure, in which the top of the head is shaved, leaving a ring of hair.

The Druids, too, shaved their heads in a certain way, for, in Celtic society, tonsures denoted to which rank of society the wearer belonged. In Ireland in the time of St. Patrick, three patterns of shaved head were recognized. They were the *airbacc giunnae*, the tonsure of the Druid; *berrad manaig*, the tonsure of the monk and priest; and *berrad magad*, the mark of the slave. In a similar way to the Druids, the Celtic monks shaved the front of their heads from ear to ear, and this tonsure was condemned by the Catholic Church as a sign of nonconformism.

RIGHT: *The Christian abbey on the sacred island of Iona, off the coast of western Scotland. The monastery was founded by St. Columba in 536.*

But the true mark of a holy person is not seen in the outward signs of dress, personal adornment or hairstyle. As the Welsh bardic *Theological Triad No 39* tells us, it is through actions and not appearance that goodness is manifested: "The three marks of a godly man: to seek after truth; to perform justice; and to exercise mercy." The Celtic saints remembered most fondly are those whose humane values shine through: those who helped the weak, sick, and poor, and showed kindness to animals.

HUMANE VALUES IN THE CELTIC CHURCH

The Celtic Church was a human institution, and like all human activities, had its good and bad points. However, among the Celtic saints are some notable humane teachers. St. David, the patron of the Welsh Church, is one of them. According to his *Life of St. David*, his Welsh biographer, Rhigyfarch recalls how: "He spent all day, never turning from his task nor wearying, in teaching and kneeling in prayer

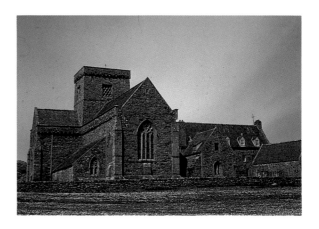

and caring for the brethren; also he fed innumerable orphans, waifs, widows, the poor, the sick, the weak, and pilgrims. So he started, so he continued, so he ended."

According to Celtic Christianity, the natural order ordained by God necessitates each member of the community supporting the others. Society can never be sustained when everyone is selfish and disregards the needs of others. In the Celtic clans as well as in the Celtic Church, mutual respect and support was the guiding principle of everyday life. It was mutuality that gave them their inner strength. This Celtic message of charity and kindness is the way that everyone can be "at home" with their neighbors and the divine. It is the teaching that contemporary Celtic Christians follow.

Many pagan Celts tattooed their bodies with the symbols of their gods as acts of homage and also in affirmation of their tribal identity.

The Celtic spiritual way asserts that we must perform every activity in life in a mindful way. There is no part of life from which the spiritual dimension ought to be excluded. In this all-inclusive Celtic world-view, there are spiritual possibilities in all things. Celtic religion thus provides meditations and prayers for every aspect of life. Some come in the form of poems or songs, while others are expressed only by deeds and actions in the physical world.

An example of this Celtic spiritual mindfulness comes in the ancient text called *The Mode of Taking Food and Drink*. It comes from the ancient Welsh writing, *The Rudiments of Divinity*: "When thou takest thy food, think of Him who gives it, namely, God, and whilst thinking of His Name, with the word put the first morsel in thy mouth, thank God for it, and entreat His grace and blessing upon it, that it may be for the health of thy body and mind; then thy drink in the same manner. And upon any other thing or quantity, which thy canst not take with the Name of God in thy mind, entreat His grace and blessing, lest it should prove an injury and a curse to thee." In Celtic spirituality, every act, even mundane, everyday tasks, can express the sacred. Worship of the divine is not just restricted to church or moments of prayerfulness.

CELTIC VALUES

The Welsh Bardic Theological Triad No 64 *tells us:*
"The three signs of a just man:
to love truth; to love peace; and to love an enemy."

CELTIC MONASTERIES

The early Celtic hermitages were in remote places, the monks lived in caves or erected basic stone huts. When monks decided to live together, the monasteries were loose aggregations of cells. In the year 563, St. Columba left Ireland and settled on the island of Iona. The monastery he founded there, and the rule for monks that he devised, became the model for Celtic monastic life.

After less than 200 years, the largest Celtic monastery was at Bangor on Belfast Lough in Ulster. Said to house 3,000 monks, Bangor was a center from where missionaries spread as far as central Europe. By the seventh century, there were large Celtic monasteries in Ireland and Great Britain, and from there missions spread out to mainland Europe. St. Sinell, a monk from Bangor, traveled from Ireland to

LEFT: *A 12th-century illuminated manuscript depicts St. Cuthbert first praising God in the sea (left), after which his feet are dried by otters (right).*

set up the monasteries of Luxeuil in France, and Bobbio, near Milan, Italy. His pupil, St. Columbanus, followed in his footsteps as one of the most adventurous missionaries of the Celtic Church. As his base in mainland Europe, he founded a monastery at Luxeuil, in the old Celtic sacred land of the Vosges in what is now eastern France. Later, he moved on to found another monastery at Fontaines, and then at Bobbio in the Italian Apennines.

PARCH

St. David taught that harmonious relationships between humans can only come into being when we have parch, *that is, respect, for each other and for the divine power.*

It was a period of very intense activity, for in a few years, Columbanus and his followers set up in the region of one hundred monasteries. They included the influential centers of learning at St. Gall, St. Bertin, Chelles, Jouarre, Jumièges, Noirmoutier, St. Riquier, and

St. Govan's Chapel, near Bosherston, Dyfed, in Wales. St. Govan may be associated with Gawain, whose tomb is said to lie under the chapel's altar.

Remirement. In mainland Europe, the old Celtic heartland, the monks selected the most favorable sites for their monasteries. Among the others was the monastic island of Reichenau in Lake Constance, a place with a wonderful climate for growing apples and other fruit, a perfect "Avalon." The Celtic monks also traveled long distances by sea, both between existing religious settlements and in search of new, isolated places. Irish priests set up religious houses in the Orkneys and Shetland Islands, from where they colonized the uninhabited Faeroe Isles some time after the year A.D. 700. They and their descendants lived there until around 860, when they were expeled by Scandinavian invaders. In the 790s, sailing Irish churchmen discovered Iceland, but made no permanent settlements there.

An exquisite representation of the Evangelist St. Matthew, accompanied by his symbol of a winged man, from the Lindisfarne Gospels.

Although the Celtic Church spread so wide, as far south as Italy and as far east as Austria, it never had the influence of the Roman Church. Celtic monasteries competed with Roman Catholic ones, and, because the Benedictine Rule of the Roman Church was less rigorous than that of St. Columbanus, the Celts lost out. Eventually, some Celtic monasteries gave up the unequal struggle and adopted some of St. Benedict's principles. Increasingly, the Roman Church put pressure on the Celts to come into line over the date of Easter and other customs.

THE FALL OF THE CELTIC CHURCH

The Celtic Church came into conflict with the Roman Catholic Church in Anglo-Saxon England in the mid-seventh century. King Oswiu of Northumbria resolved to sort out the problem, and in A.D. 664, he convened a high-level church meeting at the monastery of Steaneshalch (Whitby). King Oswiu accepted the centralist arguments put forward by the Catholic faction, and he ruled that Celtic Christianity be immediately replaced by Roman Catholicism. Those Celtic priests who would not become Catholics were banished

LIFE AT IONA

The English monk, Bede, writing in the eighth century, tells us how life in the Iona monastery was notable for its "purity of life, love of God, and faithfulness to the monastic rule."

from Anglo-Saxon territory. In the year 670, following the Synod of Whitby ruling, a synod convened at Autun in France made the Benedictine rule compulsory in French monasteries, and the Celtic rule was abolished there. These two synods sounded the death-knell of the Celtic Church.

Removed from their Celtic roots, the Celtic-founded monasteries in mainland Europe soon lost their special identity. Despite the prohibition of Celtic Christianity among the Anglo-Saxons and Picts, the Celtic Church continued to flourish in Scotland, Ireland, and Brittany. In the eighth century a reformed Celtic spiritual movement, known as the Culdees, arose partly in response to Catholic pressure. For a long period, the Culdees successfully maintained Celtic Christendom in Ireland and Scotland, and even entered England to preach and practice. But in 816, Culdees were legally prevented from prac-ticing as priests in England. However, Celtic priests worshiped in the church of St Peter in York until 936.

RIGHT: The sculpted figure of St. Hervé (right) that adorns the church of St. Anne-la-Palud at Finisterre, Brittany.

In Brittany, the Celtic Church flourished until 818, when Emperor Louis the Pious gained control. The Catholic emperor ordered that all monasteries in Brittany should abandon all Celtic practices at once, and become part of the Benedictine Order. In Scotland and Cornwall, however, Celtic usages continued.

Cornwall was conquered by King Athelstan in 925, and Catholic worship replaced the Celtic Church. However, Celtic worship continued unofficially until well into the twelfth century. In Scotland, the Celtic Church was officially abolished in 1069 by King Malcolm Canmore at his wife's suggestion. Again, this did not stop an unofficial Celtic Church from continuing. At the city of St. Andrew's, the Culdees continued to use part of the church until they were removed in 1124. Even then, in remote areas, isolated cells of Scots monks continued to use Celtic liturgies until the fourteenth century. In Ireland, The Holy Fire of St. Brigid at Kildare in Ireland, a remnant of ancient Celtic religion, was extinguished in 1220.

A depiction of the Irish St. Brendan's
mythical meeting at sea with the unhappy
Judas – a stained-glass window
designed by Harry Clarke.

CHAPTER 7

THE SACRED YEAR

THE ANCIENT CELTS had knowledge of all of the useful arts and sciences. As teachers and practitioners, the Druids were renowned for their expertise in astronomy and calendar-making. The common people, too, were familiar with the names of the stars, and how to tell the time by looking at the heavens. The Welsh Bard, Amergin, said:

"Who telleth the ages of the Moon, if not I?
Who showeth the place where the sun goes to rest,
if not I?"

This astronomical knowledge was not only practical, for it had a spiritual dimension that reflected the human place in the cosmos. The Welsh Bards taught that "There are three kinds of stars: fixed stars, which keep their places… erratic stars, which are called planets, and are fifteen in number, seven being always visible, and eight invisible … and the third are irregular stars, which are called comets, and nothing is known of their place, number and time, nor are they themselves known, except on occasions of chance, and in the course of ages." The seven visible planets

RIGHT: *The boat-shaped, corbelled stone Gallarus Oratory in Dingle, County Kerry, Ireland. Clochans such as this were used by early Christian holy men.*

were mentioned in a poem by Taliesin, *Canu y Byd Mawr* (*The Song of the Great World*). According to Bardic tradition, the eight invisible planets only appear very occasionally in a long cycle of time.

The Welsh astronomers recognized thirty-seven constellations, most of which do not coincide with the more familiar ones used today. They include the Great Plow-tail, and the Small Plow-tail, that can be paralleled with Ursa Major and Ursa Minor, but the others are quite different, being named after episodes or individuals from Celtic myth and history. They include Arthur's Harp, The Circle of Arianrod, The Circle of Gwydion, The Palace of Don, The Grove of Blodeuwedd, The Chair of

Teyrnon, The Cauldron of Ceridwen, The Soldier's Bow, and Beleiddyd's Lever. This highly developed astronomical knowledge enabled the Druids to draw up accurate calendars, and the Celtic sailors to perform great feats of navigation, such as those journeys recorded in the Irish voyaging sagas of Maelduinn and St. Brendan.

RIGHT: A medieval illustration depicting St. Dunstan, the 10th-century archbishop of Canterbury, writing. The illuminated Celtic Christian manuscripts were celebrated for their beauty.

The earth and sky were also seen in poetic terms as a vast mill. The sky appears to rotate above the earth, spinning around the pole, that resembles the Celtic vertical watermill. It consisted of an under-house, through which the mill stream ran. In this were the paddles, that, connected to a vertical axle-tree, drove the upper millstone. This turned

CELTIC TIME KEEPING

The ancient Irish saga, The Intoxication of the Ulaid, *tells how they used to tell the time at night by the position of the stars:*

"It was then that the Cú Chulainn said to Lóeg, son of Ríangabur: 'Go outside good Lóeg, and look at the stars, and determine when midnight has arrived...'"

above the fixed lower millstone through which the rotating axle-tree passed. The flowing water in the under-house was seen as symbolic of the underworld. The rotating axis did not come into contact with the lower millstone, that represents the static earth of flat-earth cosmology. The rotation is transmitted to the upper millstone, that symbolizes the heavens in motion over the static earth. The Pole Star, or "Nail" is at the center of the whirling heavens, and the celestial mill grinds the flour that is scattered to make the stars.

CELTIC PERCEPTIONS OF TIME

"Three things which cannot be finite:
God, expanse, and time."
WELSH BARDIC *TRIAD*

The Celtic year recognizes the natural division of the year by the four seasons, and the times when certain activities take place, such as herding, planting, and harvest. The Celts devised calendars based upon these natural cycles. The oldest known Celtic calendar was discovered in 1897 at Coligny in France. Dating from the first century B.C., it is a number of fragments of a tablet on which the old Celtic calendar was engraved in Greek letters. It was probably made at the time when the new Roman calendar of Julius Caesar was superseding the older calendars of Europe. The Coligny calendar is lunar. It begins months at the full moon. According to Strabo, the Celtiberians offered a sacrifice to a nameless god at full moon in front of the doors of their houses, and this is in keeping with celebrating the beginning of each month, when whole households would dance the night away each full moon. In any solar year, there are 13 lunar cycles that interact with the solar year cycle, but the full moons do not coincide with the 365-day

A limestone pillar found in Germany, covered in typical Celtic designs of vegetation and human heads (the pillar is quadrangular).

solar year. The compilers of the Coligny calendar took this into consideration, devising a thirty-year system composed of five cycles of sixty-two full moons and one cycle of sixty-one full moons. Within this is the a greater cycle that takes nineteen years to come back to the same place.

As in other European calendars, the months bore names that refer to the appropriate function for the time of year. The year began in the autumn, around the end of the modern October, with the month Samonios, "Seed-Fall." At some parts of the thirty-year cycle, the next month was Mid Samonios. In the years when it was not needed, the next month was Dumannios, "The Deepest Darkness." This was followed by months called Riuros, Anagantios, and Ogronios, which mean, respectively, "Time of Coldness," "Inability to leave the house," and "Ice Time." The spring began with Cutios, "Wind Time." It was followed by Giamonios, "Showing Shoots," and Simivisionios, "Brightness Time." Midsummer was Equos, "Horse Time," a good time for traveling, with fine weather and long days. Then came the months of the harvest period, Elembiuos, "Claim Time," and Edrinios, "Arbitration Time," when the year's financial reckoning was made. Finally, the last month of the cycle was Cantlos, "Song Time," when the

LEFT: *An ancient stone structure marks the site of St. Clether's holy well. In pre-Christian times such wells were sacred to fertility goddesses.*

Bards ended their summertime traveling, and stayed at a fixed location until the next spring. Later Celtic calendars were based upon the Roman one, but the traditional festivals were still observed.

Every traditional culture in the world recognizes that there are different qualities of time, for example, certain activities are appropriate for the time when the sun is rising, and others for sunset. Every traditional Celtic festival is related to the solar time of year. Some are related to the length of the day, the midwinter celebrations of the winter solstice and Christmas coming in the shortest days of the year, with the midsummer festivities, with danves and raising *y fedwen haf*, the summer pole, on the longest day. It would be ridiculous to conduct these celebrations at any time of year other than on the correct day. The cycles of the moon do not coincide with those of the sun, so rites and ceremonies related to the moon fall on different days. Other celebrations are related more generally to the season, such as harvest ceremonies, whose timing varies each year according to when the harvest is ready.

THE EIGHT TIDES OF THE DAY

Celtic culture has two different ways of defining the day. There is the whole day, the Irish "Là," that runs from one sunset to the next. Celtic tradition also divides the day according to clock hours, in eight tides of three hours apiece. In former times, this system was used widely in northern Europe. The ancient Welsh text, *The Divisions of the Day*, tells us: "It was in this way that they formerly computed time, and the divisions of the day: they enumerated eight parts of the day, and three hours in each part ..."

Because of their legendary coming out of darkness into light, the Celts measure periods of time not by days but by nights. When they celebrated birthdays, the first day of each month, and the New Year, they followed the rule that night precedes day. Remnants of this exist today in the English "fortnight" (fourteen nights). It is also remembered at festivals like May Eve and Christmas Eve.

UNLUCKY AND LUCKY DAYS

European tradition tells that there are certain days of the year that are lucky, and others that are unlucky. It is considered unwise to do certain things on unlucky days, for instance, going on a journey or beginning a project. Like all ancient medics, the Welsh Physicians of Myddfai treated any illness or ailment according to astrology and the calendar. They wrote: "Thirty-two days in the year are dangerous … whosoever is born on one of those days, will not live long, and whosoever is married on one of them, will die ere long, or will only exist in pain and poverty, And whosoever shall begin business on one of them, will not complete it satisfactorily."

Certain days were special because they were associated with goddesses or gods. In Ireland, the goddess Aíne was worshiped at a festival on Midsummer Day, while the god Lugh was honored at Lughnassadh, August 1. When paganism was supplanted, the Christian religion took over the older tradition. Each

RIGHT: *An illustration taken from a medieval codex depicts St. Brendan sternly resisting the temptation posed by a beautiful siren.*

TIDES OF THE DAY

The Welsh version of the eight tides is as follows. We may begin at Dewaint, the Tide of Midnight, that runs from 10.30 pm until 1.30 am. Midnight itself, like midday, falls at the middle of the Tide. Next comes Pylgeint (Dawning), from 1.30 am until 4.30 am; Bore (Morningtide), from 4.30 until 7.30 am; and Anterth (The Tide of Vapourlessness), from 7.30 till 10.30 am. The tide of Nawn (Noontide) runs from 10.30 am until 1.30 pm. It is followed by Echwydd (Rest), from 1.30 until 4.30 pm. Next comes Gwechwydd (Eventide or Twilight), from 4.30 until 7.30 pm. The final tide is Ucher (Overcast or Disappearance), that runs from 7.30 until 10.30 pm, when it is followed by Dewaint.

important saint was allocated a special day, upon which celebrations took place. Some continued the old pagan observances, like St. Brigid's Day, February 2, that took over the older festival of the goddess Brigid. Sunday became a day of rest and prayer.

Folk religion, too, continued to observe the new saints' days in the old pagan way, with garlands, bonfires, feasting, song, and dance. The festal year enabled people to be in harmony with the passing of the seasons, integrating their lives with nature. This contrasts markedly with the present-day attitude, that increasingly ignores the distinction between holy and profane days, even between day and night.

THE EIGHTFOLD YEAR

"A foggy winter, a frosty spring, a varied summer, a sunny autumn – that is a good year."

OLD IRISH PROVERB

In the twentieth century, Celtic enthusiasts recognized that an eightfold calendar could be constructed, based upon Welsh, Scottish, and Irish festivals. This is the eightfold calendar used today by many pagans and followers of Celtic traditions. However, before the Christian calendar was introduced, the ancient British way of time-reckoning recognized three divisions of the year. Firstly, there is the time of Summer, that runs from Cyntevin (March 9, Old Style) to the Calend of October (October 1). Next comes Winter, that runs from the

calend of October, to the Calend of February (February 1). Finally, the third season is Spring, that runs from the Calend of February to Cyntevin. The passing of the Celtic year in Britain was marked traditionally by four festivals called the "four points of the sun," the Albans, or Primary Points. These are the equinoxes and the solstices. Alban Elved, the point of reaping time, is the autumnal equinox. Before the change in the calendar from Old Style to New Style in 1752, the festival of the autumnal equinox, Alban Elved, fell on the Calend of

ABOVE: *The sun rises over the Bronze Age Callanish standing stones on the Isle of Lewis. They are thought to be aligned with the midsummer sun.*

to receive gifts of the three tributes of endowment, which are, corn, milk and honey." (*Barddas: Theology.*)

Other ancient Celtic festivals were not marked by significant positions of the sun, and the new year was celebrated at different times. *John Jones's Almanack*, published in Wales in 1752, states that in ancient times, before the days of Prydain, the year began at Alban Arthuan, that then fell on December 9. In Ireland, the new year was long celebrated at the festival of Oíche Shamhna and Là Shamhna, now known as Samhain. This is taken as the beginning of the eightfold year. The next festival in the eightfold year is the day

October (October 1). Alban Arthuan, "the point of roughness," is the shortest day, the winter solstice. In the Old Style before 1752, it fell at the Calend of January (New Year's Day). The next Alban is "the point of regeneration," Alban Eilir, falling on the vernal equinox. The final Alban, Alban Hevin, is the "point of summer," the summer solstice.

"There are three common feasts, according to the order and regulation of the Bards of the Isle of Britain: the first, the feasts of the four Albans; the second, the feasts of worship, at the quarters of the Moon; the third, the feasts of country and nation, and held under the proclamation and notice of forty days … it is the privilege of Bards to preside at them, and

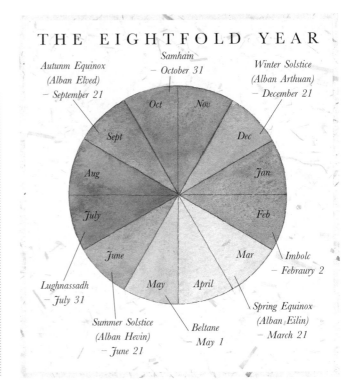

THE EIGHTFOLD YEAR

Autunm Equinox
(Alban Elved)
– September 21

Samhain
– October 31

Winter Solstice
(Alban Arthuan)
– December 21

Imbolc
– Febraury 2

Spring Equinox
(Alban Eilin)
– March 21

Beltane
– May 1

Summer Solstice
(Alban Hevin)
– June 21

Lughnassadh
– July 31

of Alban Arthuan, the winter solstice. After that comes St. Bridget's Day, which falls on February 2, the same day as the more widespread Christian festival of Candlemas. This is known as the festival of Oimelc or Imbolc, that marked the end of winter in the old Welsh calendar. Following Imbolc is the spring equinox, Alban Eilir. May Day, Là Bealtaine, anglicized as Beltane, is the first day of summer in many parts of the British Isles. It is the time of erecting the maypole, and burning the purifying balefires. Midsummer's Day is the next festival, Alban Hevin, which precedes the festival of the first harvest, Là Lúnasa or Lammas, when the first loaf of the new harvest was offered on the altars. Next comes the autumnal equinox, Alban Elved, and then the eightfold year ends again at Samhain.

ABOVE: *King Arthur and his knights are seen seated around the Round Table, at whose center is the Holy Grail.*

SAMHAIN

Samhain marks the change from summer into winter and was the time when beasts were slaughtered, if they could not be kept alive during the hard winter months. This festival is now associated with Hallowe'en or All Saints' Day, since it was also concerned with the rites of the dead. It was a feast of peace and friendship, when warriors sheathed their swords.

Although, so far as can be known, the ancient Celts never celebrated this eightfold year, as a contemporary recognition of the Celtic cycle, it is supremely appropriate.

"Do not make a custom, and do not break a custom."
OLD IRISH PROVERB

THE FESTIVALS

WINTER

In ancient Ireland, the year began at Samhain. This is Winter's Eve, called in Welsh, *Nos Galan gaeaf.* This day marks the beginning of the cold part of the year, when the declining light is very noticeable. Samhain was the Celtic festival of the dead, celebrated with ceremonial bonfires. By burning an effigy of the sorrows and terrors of the past year, the people got rid of the old and brought in the new. To the ancient Celts, this day was also a time of amnesty and free passage. At Tara, the royal center of Ireland, Samhain was celebrated by a festival that lasted for seven days. The actual feast day was in the middle of the week.

Because it is the change of the year, Samhain is an "eerie" time when the worlds of the living and the dead come together for a brief moment. Here, the division between the worlds of the living and dead is thin, and the Christianized festival of Samhain, Hallowe'en, is a time when demons, evil spirits, witches, and

RIGHT: *The Lia Fail inauguration stone on the Hill of Tara in County Meath, Ireland, where Samhain was celebrated.*

ghosts are believed to be abroad. As the Christian festival of All Saints' and All Souls' Days, it is a time when the souls of the departed are honored. In Scotland and Wales in former times, it was traditional to light the *samhnag* bonfire on Winter's Eve, though the custom has now been assimilated with Bonfire Night (Guy Fawkes' Night, November 5th).

Because Winter's Eve is a time when the normal rules do not apply, it is traditional to appear in weird disguise. This includes the wearing of masks, straw, and rush hats, going with faces blackened, or cross-dressing. A cryptic old Welsh song for *Nos Galan gaeaf* expresses the eerie nature of this night:

"Winter's Eve, Bait the apples.
Who is coming out to play?
A white lady atop the tree,
Carving an umbrella stick.
One O'Clock, Two O'Clock,
It's time for the pigs to eat."

FORETELLING
the FUTURE

Winter's Eve is the time when it is easiest to divine the future with the aid of spirits, using apples, candles, or nuts to foretell the fortunes of people in the forthcoming year. Another method used at Samhain is pouring molten lead or wax into water. The shapes it makes can be interpreted.

The Winter Solstice, Alban Arthuan, marks the death and rebirth of the sun, the day when it comes above the horizon for its shortest time, when it rises and sets farthest to the south, and has its lowest elevation at midday. Traditionally, the solstice is a time of celebration, when the light has reached its lowest ebb and is beginning to come back. In recognition of this, a log of ash or oak is ritually burned. Its ashes and charcoal are scattered in the fields to promote fertility. As with Samhain, the midwinter festivities extend for several days around the festival, especially Christmas Day and New Year's Day.

Many religions celebrate the birth of their founder around the Winter Solstice. After celebrating the birth of Jesus on March 28 for some centuries, Christians chose to come into line with the worshipers of the gods Dionysos and Mithras and so Christmas became December 25. In Celtic countries on the day after Christmas, it was customary to hunt a wren, "the king of the birds," and to carry it around the village in a box bedecked with ribbons. This ensured "joy, health, love, and peace" for the forthcoming year. In Scotland, the festival of Hogmanay, New Year, is still more powerful than Christmas.

SPRING INTO SUMMER

Celebrated at the beginning of February, Imbolc or St. Brigid's Day, L' fhéill Brighde, indicates the first stirring of the seeds in the ground, and the production of milk from the sheep with lambs. This Celtic holy day became known as Candlemas, the Christian festival of the

LEFT: *Druids used a golden sickle (foreground) to cut mistletoe from oak trees at Samhain, when two white bulls were also sacrificed.*

Purification of the Blessed Virgin Mary, celebrated by lighting torches or candles at midnight. Fire is the element of Brigid. At her shrine in Kildare, a perpetual flame was tended by nineteen nuns. At Imbolc, we enter the spring quarter of the year, the growing light being symbolized by Pagan torch and Christian candle alike. It was on this day of new beginnings that the old Scottish year began. An old Irish proverb tells us: 'Every second day is good from my day forward,' says Brigid. 'Every day is good from my day forward,' says Patrick.' Falling on or around March 21, the vernal equinox, Alban Eilir, is traditionally known as the first day of spring, when the days become longer than the nights. Unlike the foregoing festivals, Easter falls on different dates each year. The day is decided by complex calculations based on when the full moon falls in relation to the spring equinox. The variability of Easter led to the downfall of the Celtic Church, who celebrated it on a different date from that of the Roman Catholic Church. It was this difference that led finally to the Synod of Whitby in A.D. 664 that forced the Celtic

ABOVE: *A winter-solstice sunrise at Stonehenge. The Alban Arthuan was believed to involve the sun's death and rebirth.*

ST. BRIGID'S DAY

In Ireland, St. Brigid's Crosses are woven from rushes or straw and hung up in houses on this day as protective charms. It is believed that a piece of cloth or ribbon left out of doors on St. Brigid's Day gains curative powers. Offerings of food for the saint are also left outside the house.

Church to come into line with the practices of the Roman Catholic Church.

May Day, Là Bealtaine or Beltane, is traditionally the first day of summer. This is the time of mystical union, when the plants are in full growth and harmony with their environment. In former times it was the custom in Celtic countries to extinguish all of the neighborhood's fires at sunset on the eve of May Day so that the element of fire would be absent through that night. At sunrise, a new fire was made ritually, kindling it with a wooden spindle turned in a wooden socket.

RIGHT: *A later representation of a medieval reenactment of Christ vanquishing Satan, which symbolizes the victory of light over darkness.*

From this, the Beltane or Need-Fire was lit from wood of nine different types of tree. It burned on the middle of a square of nine turfs, the eight around it having been removed. People would jump through the flames to be purified. Sometimes, two fires were lit, between which farm animals were driven. Each household would take fire from the Beltane Fire and relight their hearth from it.

Because of its direct, earthy power of sexuality and growth, it was not assimilated so easily by the Church as were some other Celtic pagan festivals, and it retains its link with the god of light, Beli or Belenos. Traditionally, May Day is a time of merriment and sexual pleasures, when the May Queen is crowned to oversee the festivities. In England, the morris

dancers begin their summer dancing by dancing up the sun at sunrise on May Day. It is traditional to decorate houses with blossom and branches around the doors to bring good fortune in summer, and to set up May bushes or maypoles, around which people dance.

THE DECLINING SUN

Alban Hevin, Midsummer's Day, has the longest day and shortest night of the year. The sun rises and sets at its most northerly points, is above the horizon for the longest time, and attains its highest elevation in the sky. Midsummer sunrise is the direction of the major orientation of many stone circles, the most famous of which is Stonehenge. In Ireland, the goddess of love, Áine, was honored by celebrations on midsummer eve.

Like May Day, whose name Beltane comes from the old Celtic god Belenos, the pre-Christian name Lughnassadh comes from the god of craftsmanship and wisdom, Lugh. Celebrated on August 1, Lughnassadh or Lammas marks the beginning of the harvest, and the baking of the first loaf. This festival symbolizes the fruition of the yearly cycle in the slaughter of "John Barleycorn." Annona, deity of abundant harvest, is the goddess honored at this time. Lughnassadh marks the end of maturity and the onset of decline towards death in winter. It is a time of gathering-in where the results of hard work are harvested. Thus it symbolizes the time in the life of a craftsperson, who, after years of study and practice, finally gains the benefits of their labor, that is mastery of the craft. In former times, Lammastide was celebrated by the great hiring fairs, when the carefree joys of merry-making and sports would be combined with the serious business of taking on workers for the coming year.

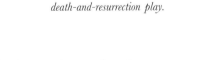

At Christmas, mummers all over England act the death-and-resurrection play.

Alban Elved is the Autumnal Equinox, when the light half of the year gives way to the dark. This is the harvest festival, the ripened achievement of the enterprise of agriculture.

ALL THE YEAR ROUND

Many customs are kept by groups of people who hand on the traditions from generation to generation. Often, and there is a degree of secrecy about their activities. On the right day, they appear in public to conduct their ceremonies. Among the performers of Celtic seasonal festivities are the Christmas Mummers, the Wren-Boys of Boxing Day, and the Pace-Eggers of Eastertime. They wear special costumes, and play music and sing songs that are only performed for the ceremony. Wearing shape-shifting costumes, putting on masks, or coloring the face are the means of stepping out of individual identity into the collective.

The twelve days of Christmas are the traditional time for the outings of the Border morris dancers. Wearing costumes made of multicolored tatters, with their faces blackened, and carrying fearsome staves, the morris men perform dances that drive out evil and bring good luck. On May Day it is customary for certain people to dress in green leaves and become Jack-in-the-Green and dance around the maypole. Then, also, guisers dress in ritual animal disguise and dance among the revelers. Most ceremonies are performed whether or not there are any spectators, for the performance itself is the important thing, "keeping up the day."

CHAPTER 8

CELTIC LANDSCAPES

THE LAND IS THE NURTURER of all human life. Without a grounding in the soil, human culture has no basis. Everything to do with Celtic culture is bound up with the landscape. In Celtic countries, the land is alive with myth, history, and holiness. Folk-wisdom teaches that whenever we acknowledge the spirit of any place, then we can bring forth divine ideals there. When the land is in good order spiritually, then order-liness will reign in human society.

Stonehenge is probably the most sacred of all Celtic holy places.

There will be peace and plenty, the fields, flocks, and herds will flourish.

At holy places, we can become aware of the intimate relationships between humans, deities, nature, and our ancestors. Universal divinities can also be recognized as being present at a holy place. They include elemental divinities, such as the spirits of water, earth, thunder, and air, personifications of the Earth Mother, and conceptual deities such as the goddesses and gods of wealth and peace. Imported deites may also be recognized at a particular place. These are the gods and goddesses that originated in other places, even other lands, although their principles can be recalled at the holy place.

ANIMA LOCI

A Celtic holy place may be honored by the worship of a holy being there. It may be a manifestation of the Anima Loci or place-soul, present in a tree, stone, or spring. Departed human beings who once lived on Earth, celebrated as saints or heroes, can also be honored at specific places. According to Celtic beliefs, the human and the divine are aspects of the same reality. The stream of life, of which we, and the animal and plant kingdoms are part, also includes the world of spirit. We have the same origin and nature as angelic and godly beings, and, like them, are entitled to equal respect.

CELTIC FIELDS

The ancient agricultural remains called Celtic fields can still be seen in many parts of Britain. They are square or rectangular in shape, and vary in area from one-third to one-and-a-half acres. The size was the amount of land that could be plowed in a day, and varied according to the kind of terrain. In places, they form hillside terraces known as lynchets, in perfect

The chalk outline of the Cerne Abbas giant, in Dorset, England. A clear fertility symbol, it is speculated that the giant was the site of Beltane rituals.

harmony with the landscape, preventing soil erosion down the slope. In less favorable terrain, the Celtic "lazybed" is a system of horticulture that brings fertility to barren land. Good soil is transported to rocky land, where it is laid within enclosures bordered by rocks, creating fertile strips between one and three yards wide, oriented appropriately for the land where they are made. To the soil is added local peat, crushed seashells, and seaweed. This composts to make an exceptionally good growing compound. Through the sheer hard work of making "lazybeds," the Celtic farmers extended the fertility of the Earth, which is a sacred act. "Lazybeds" were made on barren islands by Celtic monks and, in later years, by crofters' families deported to uninhabited islands during the Highland Clearances. Today, "lazybeds" are cultivated on the islands of Eriskay and Scalpay in the Inner Hebrides as well as in the west of Ireland.

TREES IN THE CELTIC LANDSCAPE

The Druids worshiped in forest groves, and venerated particular oak trees that had been marked by lightning by the god Taranis. A lone holy tree called Bile grew at any sacred place where Celtic kings were inaugurated. The French town of Billom is such a place, "the

RIGHT: *The trees of Glencoe, in the Scottish Highlands, were once part of the vast Wood of Caledon. The Celts recognized the sanctity of such forests, and therefore venerated them.*

plain of the holy tree." There were five of these holy trees in Ireland, one in each province. Holy trees are believed to protect the area where they grow. It is traditional to honor trees by decking them with rags, ribbons, or flags. Ancient tree-dressing ceremonies are still conducted in a number of places in England. During the midsummer ceremony of "Bawming the Thorn Tree" at Apperley in Cheshire, the hawthorn tree is bedecked with red ribbons. At Aston-on-Clun, in Shropshire, colorful flags adorn the sacred poplar tree throughout the year, being renewed each May.

The pagan Celts worshiped their goddesses and gods in sacred groves, called *nemeton*, "clearings open to the sky." These were enclaves in woodland, powerful sacred places, entered only by priests and priestesses. They worshiped in the open without temples. At least some holy groves were dedicated to specific deities. Dio Cassius tells that the Britons worshiped at groves where they revered Andraste, goddess of victory. Other goddesses worshiped in groves include the two goddesses of the *nemeton*, Arnemetia and Nemetona, and Belesama. In France, the name of the city of Nanterre recalls the Celtic "Nemetodunum." In Britain, the sites of Vernemeton, "the especially

MERLIN'S OAK

Before it was removed to widen a road, Merlin's Oak at Carmarthen in Wales was linked to the town's well-being: "When Merlin's Tree shall tumble down, Then shall fall Carmarthen town."

sacred grove," and Medionemeton, "the middle sanctuary," are known. When Christianity was introduced, some holy woods were cut down, and others came under the protection of Celtic saints. In Wales, trees growing on land sacred to St Beuno were protected. No one was allowed to cut or damage them in any way.

Although Christian monks often cut down pagan holy trees, apple orchards were spared, and new ones planted. The *Liber Landavensis* records that in sixth-century Brittany, the British monks Teilo and Samson "planted a great grove of fruit-bearing trees, to the extent of three miles, from Dôl as far as Cai." To this day, St. Teilo is the patron of apple trees.

Some Celtic forests were holy throughout, among them the Forest of Brocéliande in Brittany and the Wood of Caledon in Scotland. Among the remains of Brocéliande are the Forêt de Huelgoat, the Forêt de Paimpont, and Coat-an-Hay and Coat-an-Noz.

LEFT: *Elizabeth Forbes's atmospheric painting,* King Arthur's Wood. *The spirits of legendary Celtic heroes like Arthur and Merlin were often associated with specific trees or groves.*

LANDS OF
THE ANCESTORS

Ancestral holy places, the collective shrines of the Celtic community, were administered by the families who legally owned them. Celtic common law dictated that land could not be bought and sold. The only way that the ownership of land could change was through inheritance. The families priests were drawn from were also landowners of the most holy places in the landscape. When the change came from paganism to Christianity, any man who changed his religion maintained his family's legal rights over its ancestral holy places. This meant that when the head of a family was converted to the Christian religion, then its ancestral holy places were also available for the

use of the new religion. Because of this rule, many ancient Celtic monasteries are on places of former pagan sanctity. Even when churches were founded on new sites, they were still on the ancestral land.

The medieval *Lives* of many Celtic saints tell of many kinds of magical acts they performed to find appropriate places for churches or religious settlements. They used various

SACRED ORCHARDS

Ancient apple orchards are Celtic sacred groves. In Wales and western England, the apple trees are wassailed in the wintertime with songs, offerings of bread and drink, and guns fired into the air to ward off evil in the coming year. Orchards are protected under ancient Celtic law. The British Free Miners of Cornwall, Devon, and the Forest of Dean, are allowed to prospect and extract coal and minerals from their areas. The royal charters of the Free Miners have precedents in ancient Welsh law. They give the miners the right to dig on any land, except the king's highway, churchyards, and orchards. To dig the ground there is sacrilegious.

both from the pagan Celtic tradition and from the Etruscan principles taught by the college of Roman field surveyors called *Agrimensores*. The same omens and portents, which in pagan times were studied by the Vates, were noted by the priests of the Celtic Church, and used in the choice of sites for new chapels and monasteries.

The intimate Celtic relationship with the land, expressed through myth and legend, exists equally in the pagan and Christian traditions. The same animals led pagan heroes and Christian saints to special places, and the same methods were used to enclose and consecrate the land. Time and space are linked in Celtic tradition. There are a number of legends that tell how a large area of land was taken in a day. When St. Hoiernin asked the local lord at Quelen in Brittany to give him some land for his monastery, the lord offered him as much land as he could dyke round in a single day. So St Hoiernin walked all day around a large tract of land, trailing his staff along the ground, leaving a boundary mark. This was considered as valid a boundary marker as a ditch and bank around the area, and the saint was given the land. Other monastic boundaries required only a walk around them to make them legal. One day's walk by the pet deer of St. Elian the Pilgrim around Caswallon's land defined his monastic estate.

LEFT: *Glastonbury Tor is linked in legend with King Arthur. The Holy Grail was said to have been thrown into the Chalice Well at its foot.*

techniques of geomancy to find suitable places, taking heed of dreams, revelations, and omens. Their chapels, hermitages, holy wells, and stopping-places were the same traditional places of power recognized in heathen tradition. These techniques of location were not newly developed by Christian priests, but were the same as those used by the Vates and Roman pagans. These specific techniques came

HOLY TRACKS
AND ROYAL ROADS

The Celtic pathfinders who made the old trackways had a supremely intimate knowledge of the landscape, giving them moderate gradients, making them avoid hillcrests and crossing rivers at the easiest fords. Celtic

empowerment. These markers enabled the wayfarer to find his or her way without getting lost physically or spiritually during the journey. Many such monastic trackways with breathtaking waymarkers remain in the Black Mountains of mid-Wales, on Dartmoor in western England, and in the Wicklow Mountains of Ireland.

trackways are punctuated by easily visible holy stopping-places, which are marked by cairns, isolated boulders, stone crosses, wayside chapels, and thorn trees. The pious wayfarer would stop at each of these waymarkers in turn and say a prayer of thanks or

LEFT: An illustration inspired by Thomas Grey's poem, The Bard, who cursed the English army before throwing himself off the cliff.

The ancient Celtic trackways are physical instances of the spiritual ways in the material world. Some were made for everday use, while others were holy roads linking sacred places. These were made specially for pilgrims and priests to use.

ABOVE: Lancelot and a fellow knight relax in the company of dancers. Many Celtic sacred sites are associated with Arthurian legend.

The early Celts were famed for their fine wheeled vehicles, that meant that there had to be roads on which to run them. Before the Romans came, there were the roads of the amber trade that ran from southern Europe to the Baltic shore. Areas of Europe never ruled by Rome, such as Ireland, also possess ancient roads, made by highly skilled road-builders. Bardic tradition in Britain tells of certain roads that were the king's direct responsibility – the Four Royal Roads of Britain. According to legendary history, these four roads were built by the order of two Celtic kings of Britain, Dunwal Molmutius and his son Belinus. They were built for the free use of people of "all nations and foreigners." The roads were given the same sanctity as rivers and sanctuaries, they were regarded as places of worship and free passage was guaranteed for everybody. Everyone who traveled on the royal roads was walking on holy ground, and thus under the legal protection of the king. The sacred status of the British royal roads was confirmed several times in laws passed by later, non-Celtic, monarchs. We can still travel along Watling Street, the Fosse Way, the Icknield Way, and Ermine Street today, which are main roads.

A stone pillar being carved with the symbols of the Ogham tree-alphabet. Celts erected standing stones to identify a landscape as being sacred.

Medieval Ireland also possessed royal roads. There were five of them, radiating from the royal center at Tara. They are called Slige Midluachra, Cualann, Dala, Asal, and Mór. Slige Mór, the Midwest Road, links the royal center at Tara with the sacred center of Ireland at Uisnech. Some of the ancient Irish roads were sacred. A causeway over seven miles long, called Casan na Naomh, "The Pathway of the Saints," runs over hilly and boggy terrain in County Kerry between St. Brendan's Mountain and Kilmakedar church. The Irish tracks are mostly named after Christian saints, but the Celtic royal road on the Isle of Man is named for the legendary king, Orry.

THE FOUR DIRECTIONS AND THE CENTER

As they were long-distance travelers by both land and sea, it is not surprising that the Celts have a sophisticated understanding of direction. The airts, or the points of the compass, each have their own particular character, defined by the winds which blow from them. In the east is the purple wind; to the south, the wind is white; to the west, the wind is pale in color, and to the north, the wind is black.

The qualities of these winds were general principles for locating things, such as orienting buildings in the most favorable way. The Celts considered the "black wind" of the north to be a bad direction. Medieval Cornish miracle plays were performed at permanent circular earthworks called *Plen an Gwary*, which were arranged so that different characters occupied the directions that reflected their character. These directions had symbolic meanings which were reflected in Celtic lore. Bad or pagan characters are grouped in the north. In the *Meryasek* play, both a demon and the god Jupiter are each called "our patron saint on the North Side."

Generally, the east represents prosperity; the south, music; the west, learning; and the north, warfare. The center, that is not a direction, but

A characteristically romantic, Pre-Raphaelite interpretation of Arthurian knights setting off on their quest for the Holy Grail, which possessed the power of healing.

SPIRITUAL WALKING

The ancient Celtic waymarkers knew that the simple necessity of going on foot can be a spiritual act. There are many allusions to spiritual walking along "the straight and narrow way," being in accordance with God's will. When one follows good advice, then one cannot get lost. "He who will not take advice will take the crooked track," is a Gaelic teaching. Keeping to the right road is a metaphor for the devotee's life journey along the road to Paradise.

a place, is kingship. To this day, Ireland retains the ancient Celtic division of land. The island is divided into five ancient provinces that represent the four airts plus the middle. Leinster is in the east of Ireland, Munster in the south, Connacht in the west, and Ulster in the north. At the center of Ireland was the old

THE FOUR AIRTS

An old Irish proverb gives the qualities of these "Four Winds of Erin:"

"The east wind is dry and puts fleece on the sheep,
The west wind is generous and puts
fish in the nets.
The south wind is moist
and makes the seeds flourish.
The north wind is harsh and makes people sad."

province of Meath, "the middle." Here was the royal center of Tara, where the High King of Ireland held court.

The Assembly of Tara was held each Samhain under the protection of the goddess Tea. It called together the rulers and aristocrats of the whole of Ireland. At the Assembly, the Ulstermen camped to the north of Tara; those from Leinster were on the east, and so on. Thus, the four quarters of Ireland were all present at the center during the festival. To Tara, the men of Leinster brought new treasures; those of Munster, new music and games. The Connacht people brought new stories and learning, while the Ulstermen demonstrated new arts of war. The layout of

their encampment reflected the symbolic geography of the whole island, with the High King at the center. The Great Hall of Tara, where the High King held court, also had a symbolic layout. The monarch was guarded by four men who surrounded him in the form of a cross. Symbolically, the High King sat at the center of his country. He was guarded in the north, east, south, and west by his army, which in turn faced enemies coming correspondingly from all four quarters. This ritual order was essential at Samhain, a festival during which the land was subject to attack by the demonic forces of the otherworld.

PLACES OF SANCTITY

The pagan Celts worshiped in *Nemetons*, clearings in woodland, where sacred trees stood. These were largely the preserve of the Druids. The *Temenos* was the major place of collective worship, being an enclosure surrounded by an earth bank and ditch. Before the Roman conquest of Gaul, there were no buildings inside sacred enclosures. Temples came later, under Roman influence. After the introduction of Christianity, the form of churchyards followed the earlier pagan principles. The circular churchyards known as *llan* in Wales and other Celtic lands are examples of this continuity. A wall, hedge, or earth bank divides the consecrated ground of the garth and the profane world outside. In some places, these churchyards are actually the old pagan holy enclosures with standing stones.

CELTIC MONASTERIES

The basic Celtic monastery was a group of small buildings surrounded by a more or less circular bank and ditch. This form still exists at a number of places in Ireland, including Clonmacnoise and Glendalough. Early Celtic monastic buildings included living places and an oratory or church for worship. Monastic enclosures also contained stone crosses and other sacred structures such as the open-air altars called leachta. Some contained the tombs of their founders and the round towers that are the most characteristic structure of Irish Celtic monasteries. The best surviving round towers are at Antrim, Ardmore, Cashel, Devenish, and Glendalough. Although primarily defensive, they also served as landmarks for wayfarers on the cross-country monastic trackways.

Standing stones are important markers of holy places in the Celtic landscape. Although the most ancient are pre-Celtic, the tradition of setting up memorial and mark-stones was continued by the Celts. Even after the introduction of Christianity, people did not stop venerating stones. Celtic priests, most notably St. Samson, traveled through the country carving crosses on old standing stones. Later Celtic priests set up stones marked with crosses, that developed gradually into the fine free-standing Celtic crosses. In parallel, it seems that people continued to erect pagan standing stones. As late as 1699, a man was charged with idol worship by the Church authorities at Elgin in Scotland. He had set up a standing stone and raised his cap to it.

Stones with crosses carved on them mark holy places in the landscape. They may be former pagan megaliths, Christianized by traveling monks. They may mark the grave of a priest or chieftain, or be stopping-places for pilgrims who wish to pray on sacred trackways. Others may mark boundaries of monastic land. As time passed, Christianized standing stones gave way to stone crosses. A great many of the early

ABOVE: A View of Loch Lomond Near Inversaid *by Alfred de Breanski. The Celts regarded such crags, groves, and lochs as being sacred.*

cross-slabs were older stones reconsecrated to the Christian religion by the addition of a cross. Later, new slabs were made and carved with wheel-crosses. Finally, after three or four centuries of cross-slabs, free-standing stone crosses were made. The high wheel-headed crosses are the most characteristic artifacts of Celtic Christianity. Over the years, new crosses became progressively larger and more elaborate. In western Scotland and Ireland, this culminated in the impressive high crosses, such as those that still stand at many ancient monastic settlements, including Ahenny, Castledermot, Clonmacnois, Moone, and Monasterboice and receive thousands of visitors today.

Lindisfarne Abbey was founded in A.D. 635 by St. Aidan. It fell into ruin after its monks fled the Vikings in 875.

HOLY WELLS, HEALING, AND THE GRAIL

The Celtic arts of healing were essentially religious, and centered at specific locations, at holy wells and healing waters. There were many goddesses and gods that ruled holy wells. Some were purely local, like Coventina, goddess of the holy well at Carrawbrough on Hadrian's Wall. Other well-deities were more widespread. In the middle Rhine and Moselle regions, Sirona was the most important goddess of healing springs and holy wells. Along with the god Grannos, she presided over a major healing shrine at Hochscheid im Hunsruck, Germany. Sulis, goddess of the healing hot springs at Bath in western England, also had holy wells in other places, including Fynnon Sul, near Kidwelly Castle in west Wales, and St. Sunday's Well in Dublin. Gwenhudw is the patroness of the holy wells in west Wales called Ffynnon Gwenhudw. There, she is known as the queen of the "little people."

The Celtic sun god, Grannos, was associated with hot springs. One of his largest shrines was at Aquae Granni, in the modern city of Aachen in western Germany. It was believed that the sun descended beneath the Earth at night, and heated the waters there, that come up in hot springs. Thus, the waters, guarded by the goddess of the well, contain the healing powers of the sun-god. The god variously called Borvo, Bormo, Bormanus, and Burmanus, whose name means "the boiler," is the most important god of hot and healing springs, having shrines in the south of France and Liguria in Italy. The tradition of well-dressing in parts of England and Germany, that continues today, is a parallel of the ancient Celtic practice of honoring curative springs.

The main shrine of the British healing-god Nodens was a temple at Lydney Park, on the banks of the River Severn in western England.

At this shrine, archeologists discovered images of dolphins, conch shells, anchors, and fishermen, linking Nodens with the waters. Many people left votive offerings at his shrine

LEFT: *St. Non's Well, near St. David's, Dyfed, in Wales. St. Non was the mother of St. David, and her well was believed to possess curative powers.*

in gratitude for cures. They depict the healed part of the body, just like modern ex-votos left by devotees at Catholic and Orthodox shrines in parts of Europe. Another water deity is the Gaulish goddess Nantosuelta, whose name refers to running water. Depicted with a horn of plenty and a dish, she is connected with a medieval story about the coming of the wasteland, and its restoration by the Holy Grail.

The healing power of the Holy Grail is connected with springs in the text called *The Elucidation*. It tells of how once holy wells were guarded by ethereal young women with golden cups. But an evil king, Amangons, raped one of the women and stole her golden chalice. Then, his men raped and robbed the other well-women, and drove them away. The once-fertile land became barren, and there was illness and famine. But all was not lost. However, one of the few remaining good knights, Blihis Blihiris, found out that the Holy Grail had the ability to reempower the wells and their female guardians. From this came King Arthur's knights' quest for the Grail, that, when found, restored the holy wells and the health and fertility of the land.

WELL DRESSING

Well dressing dates back to the ancient worship of water nymphs, who had to be placated annually so that the local water supply might continue. It is a form of picture making, incorporating natural objects such as stones, leaves, moss, rocks, wild fruit, and flower petals. Today, well-dressing generally illustrates a biblical story and takes place on the day of the saint to whom the local church is dedicated. In England it is particularly widespread in the Peak District of Derbyshire.

CHAPTER 9

THE CELTIC HERITAGE

OVER THE MILLENNIA, there has been a remarkable continuity in Celtic religion, despite several radical changes of official belief-system. The greatest change of all was from paganism to Christianity, but even this radical alteration in doctrine was accomplished smoothly with a minimum of real change. There were gains and losses when Christianity was adopted. Human sacrifice was abolished, and the sense of human justice was enhanced. Now tithes and tribute were given to the Church, and wealth accumulated there instead of being piled up as trophies or deposited in sacred lakes. The ancient customary laws were modified, admitting Christian ideas only so far as they did not interfere with ancient Celtic family and clan traditions. Neither did the ancient, customary holy places alter a great deal. New churches were built there, and the images of the old gods were embedded in the walls. The holy days of paganism were retained, although they were still rededicated to Christian saints whose ceremonies were similar to those of the deities they supplanted. But women, formerly

LEFT: *The legend of St. Non is not confined to Wales: this carving of St. David's mother stands above a sacred well in Dirinon, Brittany, in France.*

at the heart of religion, were excluded from the priesthood and often also from holy places. The institutions of slavery and cruel punishments remained in place and were not abolished by either the Celtic or the Catholic Churches.

Among the common people, a syncretic "dual faith" came into being, in which the official Christian liturgy of the Church was supplemented by vernacular customs and usages that were pagan in origin. The old gods

THE MOTHER GODDESS

The mother of the gods was known by a variety of names, including Anna, Nonna, Dona, and other versions containing the elements "nan" and "non." She was associated with the holy wells of the Celts and after their conversion to Christianity was revered as St. Anne, whose cult is still highly significant in Brittany today. Images of her that were unearthed by chance were thought to have been revealed through divine grace and subsequently became sacred objects of worship.

were not forgotten in Wales, Scotland, Ireland, and Brittany, but the essence of their worship sometimes continued under the name of a saint. Among others, the Celtic mother-goddess

Anna continued to be venerated in Christian times. In Brittany, the cult of St. Anne took over her cultus, while in Wales, it was St. Non, and in Ireland, Brigid. Occasionally, ancient pagan images were restored to use. In 1625, while working in a field at Keranna, in Morbihan, a Breton farmer named Yves Nicolazic unearthed an ancient statue of the Mother Goddess. The local Carmelite priest identified it as St. Anne. A chapel was built to house the image, and an annual pilgrimage was set up. Each July, pilgrims visit Sainte-Anne d'Auray, where a basilica was built in the 1870s. Today, up to 100,000 people go there during the pilgrimage, the largest in Brittany.

Other local deities also continued under the guise of Christianity. At Llanderfel, in Merionethshire, Wales, for example, the being called Darvel Gadarn was venerated. He had a sacred image, a sixteenth-century source tells us, "in which the people have so great confidence, hope and trust, that they come dayly a pilgrimage unto him, some with kyne, other with oxen and horses." This veneration continued until the Reformation, when the image was taken to London and burned.

The country Bards, wise women, and cunning men maintained spiritual traditions

King Arthur battles against a Roman general in this medieval French image; despite his stand, Celtic belief would ultimately be assimilated into Roman Catholicism.

long after they were ignored by conventionally learned people in the cities. Even the mystical Ogham tree alphabet, always known to but a few Bards, was never forgotten. People continued to write in Ogham on tombstones, and the tradition is not dead today. In the nineteenth century, an Irishman surnamed Collins who lived at Kinsale in County Cork always carried a walking stick on which he had painted a poem about the zodiac in white Ogham characters. He also wrote his name on his cart in Ogham, and he was prosecuted by the police for not writing it in the Roman alphabet, but was acquitted.

LATTER-DAY DRUIDRY

Although Druidism was superseded by the Celtic Church, the traditions were embedded in folk song and poetry, and never quite died out. Pagan practices continued in the vernacular religion of the countryside even when kings and lords were Christian. The exploits and doctrines of the Druids of old were retold by generations of Bards, and their sacred places were remembered and honored. Throughout the Middle Ages, knowledge of the ancient Druids was maintained. Antiquarian studies of the remains of former times became popular in

the late seventeenth century, leading to a new awareness of Celtic paganism among the learned. In 1676, in his *Britannia Antiqua Illustrata*, Aylett Sammes wrote that the Druids believed in "the Immortality of the Soul, to which they added the Transmigration of it."

According to modern Druidic historians, who are the heirs of the tradition, and guardians of the records, Celtic spirituality in England has ancient roots which were not destroyed by the Anglo-Saxons. Around the year 800, a "Grove" or lodge of the Celtic metalworkers' guild, the Pheryllt, called Cor Emrys, existed at Oxford. Druidic history tells that the uni-

Shanganagh Cromleac, a typical Celtic "fairy place," reputed abode of the "little people."

versities of Oxford and Cambridge were founded at places of traditional Celtic spiritual activity. In Oxford, a lodge of Celtic spirituality called the Mount Haemus Grove was founded (or refounded) by Haymo of Haversham in 1245 and was re-activated in around 1694 by the antiquary John Aubrey, and consolidated by John Toland in 1717. This date is counted as the foundation of modern Druidism, the same year that the worshipful craft of freemasonry was set up. There have been Druidic groups in Britain ever since.

ABOVE: *A Pre-Raphaelite interpretation of King Arthur, and the Round Table, receiving his summons.*

In the eighteenth century, there arose a renewed national awareness in the Druidic heritage, resulting in several influential books. The Reverend Henry Rowlands of Anglesey published *Mona Antiqua Restaurata* in 1723. Druidic paganism was viewed not as harmful, but as a benign awareness of harmony with Nature. Later, John Toland's book, *Christianity not Mysterious*, denied the Church's teaching that Christianity is the only true religion, claiming that the ancient Druids also had access to spiritual truth. Following John Toland, the Bardic mystic artist and poet William Blake wrote that: "The antiquities of every Nation under Heaven is no less sacred than that of the Jews. They are the same thing ..."

Also during the eighteenth century, an increased awareness of what they saw as Druidic traditions led architects to study the ancient monuments of Britain. The leading exponent of "Druidical" building was the mystical architect John Wood the Elder (1704–54) who believed that his home town, Bath, was once the "Metropolitan Seat of the Druids," with temples of the sun and moon as well as a shrine at the famous hot springs. In his book, *Choir Gaure* (1747), John Wood claimed that the great stone circle of Stonehenge was "a temple erected by the

ABOVE: *Gérard's painting,* Ossian Conjures up the Spirits on the Bank of the River Lorca. *Ossian (Oisin) was the son of Fionn mac Cumhaill.*

British Druids." As an architect, he made a significant contribution to Georgian Bath, where he applied his newly rediscovered esoteric principles according to the canons of Georgian architecture. Most notable of Wood's designs in Bath is the Circus, constructed according to the plan and proportional system he discerned at Stonehenge, and covered with symbolic emblems. His other Bath masterpiece, the Royal Crescent, reflects the lunar element of ancient Celtic philosophy.

The richly decorated Irish Ardagh Chalice is believed to date from the 8th century. It is an image of the Grail..

OSSIAN, IOLO, AND THEIR LEGACY

In the 1760s, James MacPherson published his "Ossian" poetry, which he passed off as coming from ancient manuscripts. It was an immediate success throughout Europe, depicting an ancient and noble tradition. MacPherson based his work on traditional Fenian ballads that he had collected, but greatly rewrote and embellished them. Later, MacPherson was seen as a forger, but regardless of their origin, the Ossian poems helped to rekindle an awareness of Celtic tradition. Similarly, modern Welsh culture owes a great deal to the Mason and Bard Iolo Morgannwg (Edward Williams). In a century when thinkers claimed that the traditions of past had been superseded by

modernity, Iolo promoted Celtic Bardism as a living tradition having ancient roots.

In 1792, in company with English Druids headed by David Samwell, Iolo conducted a Gorsedd of Bards on Primrose Hill, to the north of London. There, in a stone circle, Iolo set up the rituals that were later to become the core of the Welsh National Eisteddfod. However, his Druidism was not a form of Welsh nationalism, because the English and Welsh Druids there made a solemn declaration that from then onward the English language was to be considered equally authentic with Welsh for all bardic and Druidic purposes.

IOLO MORGANNWG

Iolo was a man of his time, who recast the traditional bardic knowledge of Glamorgan in a new form that was fitting for his time. In all periods of human history, there have been inspired spiritual teachers. Many have based their teachings on earlier ideas, but have been the catalyst for a new, more powerful, understanding of their tradition. Iolo Morgannwg was one of these. His collections of ancient texts, and his own inspired re-writings and additions to them, have formed the basis of modern Druidry. This "Morgannwgian Druidism" has continued unbroken for over two hundred years.

Some historians and archeologists complain that present-day Druids use copies of artifacts that come not from traditional craft but are conscious copies of old work. They see modern Celtic art as no more than an imitation that comes from an incorrect understanding of the "originals." But this is a mistake, for in the real world, everything is evolving continuously, and that is equally true for Celtic art. Whether the Druids wear replicas of Irish Bronze Age necklets, or embroidered patterns that originated in tenth-century Wales, they are authentic expressions of the contemporary Druidic identity.

Both Celtic paganism and Celtic Christianity have seen a great renewal since the 1970s. Despite persecution, neither died out completely, for elements of them continued among the countrypeople. Celtic folk-tradition preserved pagan knowledge right through the Christian era. The Fairy Faith, and knowledge of spirits have been maintained in rural Celtia until the present day. Welsh folklore tells how sensitive people can commune with departed spirits at burial mounds. Ellis Wynne's book, *Gweledigaetheu y Bardd Cwsc*, published in 1703, describes how a sleeping Bard has three visions of this world, death, and hell. In a vision of the dead, the Children of Annwn, they dance upon

The sacred pagan pillar is combined with the primary symbol of Christianity within this stone Celtic cross.

the churchyard mound. To the Celts, these mounds are not only places of burial, but can also be places of vision, where the seer may take a glimpse into the otherworldly realms. Contemporary Celtic paganism has a large spirit element.

CONTEMPORARY CELTIC PAGANISM

The restoration of Druidism as an organized force in the eighteenth century led to a search for the true roots of the faith. Scholarly studies of ancient Celtic mythology and religion provided the answers, and they were polytheistic. In the middle of the nineteenth century, Druids at the Welsh National Eisteddfod began to add prayers to pagan deities to their more general, unitarian statements. The Romantic poets, too, recognized the pagan ensoulment of the Celtic landscape. A twentieth-century poet, Robert Graves, was highly influential in restoring Celtic paganism. In his book, *The White Goddess*, he unraveled the complex mysteries of European mythology. Brilliantly, he explained the meaning of the Celtic tree-alphabet, Ogham, and instituted a Tree Calendar. Graves asserted that the return of goddess-oriented religion would rectify the imbalance of patriarchal religion that had led to modern destructivity.

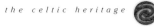

The female aspect of religion, which is implicit in Celtic paganism, attracted many women, who saw the pagan path as more relevant to them than male monotheism. They discovered that many of the traditions of the Celtic hereditary wise women, often persecuted as witches, were the continuation of valuable ancient skills and wisdom. When this knowledge was made available widely, many women and men were able to contribute to a new flowering of Celtic paganism. Since the 1970s, Celtic pagan groups

ABOVE: *This silver shield and the fragments that flank it were found in Italy, and are embossed with human heads and rams' horns – the latter symbols of fertility.*

THE EISTEDDFOD

An eisteddfod is a traditional Welsh gathering, that lasts up to a week and is dedicated to the bardic arts of music, literature, and poetry, with a strong choral and competitive element. Dating from pre-Christian times, the festival takes its name from the Welsh word eistedd, meaning "to sit." In their present form eisteddfods have taken place since 1817 and now occur annually in a number of Welsh towns. Candidates who pass various tests are conferred with the degrees of Ovate, Bard, and Chief Musician. An international eisteddfod, in which choirs and dancers from around the world compete, has been held at Llangollen since 1947.

have sprung up both in the old Celtic realms and lands where people of Celtic descent live. Following the ancient Celtic love of nature, devotees of modern Celtic paganism do not withdraw from the world and society, but are active environmentalists, using their wisdom to nurture human society and the natural world.

RIGHT: The stone situated at the end of the passageway of this cairn at Loughcrew, Ireland, is illuminated by the sun's rays at dawn on the winter solstice.

THE TARTAN RESTORATION

The eighteenth century was not a good time for Celtic traditions. Between 1747 and 1782, after the Jacobite rebellion was crushed in Scotland, the British government's "Clothing Act" was in force. It banned the weaving or wearing of tartan in the Scottish Highlands as an attempt to eliminate the rebellious clans. But although the ban was enforced with ferocity in the Highlands, it did not operate in lowland Scotland or England, and so the art of weaving plaid did not die out. Weavers continued to produce tartan cloth for the British Army and for export to the colonies. Creatively, they made new patterns, and, instead of destroying tartan, the "Clothing Act" led to a proliferation of colorful and vibrant new designs.

In the early part of the nineteenth century, attempts were made to regularize clan tartans. Colonel David Stewart asked Andrew Robertson of the Highland Society of London

to request each clan chief to send an authentic piece of his own tartan to the society, so that a register could be compiled. The Highland Society of London Certified Tartans was set up in 1816. When King George IV visited Edinburgh in 1822, clan chiefs and representatives strove to appear before the king in authentic clan tartans, and where there were no known clan tartans in existence, new ones were devised for the event. These tartans are still used by certain clans today.

The need for ceremonial clan tartans spurred further research, and a number of Scottish writers provided what was wanted. In his book, *The Scottish Gael*, published in 1831, James Logan detailed 55 clan tartans. John and Charles Allen, who used various surnames, but eventually became known as the Sobieski Stuarts, claimed to have an old manuscript that recorded details of the old and authentic clan tartans. In 1842 they published what they said was an edited version of their manuscript, under the title of *Vestiarum Scoticum*. Later tartan researchers have found that the Sobieski Stuarts' patterns were not ancient, but invented by the brothers. However, some clan tartans in use today stem from *Vestiarum Scoticum*.

The success of the Sobieski Stuarts and others consolidated tartan as the national emblem of the Scots. Where clans had no recognized distinctive tartan, new tartans were commissioned. Even the royal family designed their own, called Balmoral. Today, the established custom is that the right to wear the clan tartan is vested in those who bear the clan name. However, for those who have no right to wear a specific clan tartan, it is customary to use those allowed for general wear. These include the Royal and Hunting Stewart tartans, and the Black Watch and Caledonia patterns.

THE CELTIC RESURGENCE

A feeling that Celtic culture was in decline led many Celts to revive the tradition. As early as the late seventeenth century, John Keigwin of Mousehole in Cornwall, formed a group to preserve and promote the declining Cornish language. Thomas Tonkin, one of the group, collected and published many Cornish folk songs. In Brittany, from 1806, the vicar of Saint-Solomon parish at Vannes, Joseph Mah, researched and collected Breton traditions, including folk songs and dances. The work of these and others preserved important elements of Celtic heritage.

The Irish Book of Kells *dates from at least the 10th century. Its striking Christian imagery is beautifully embellished by traditional Celtic motifs drawn from the natural world.*

The Jacobite rebellions and the subsequent repression of Highland culture after 1746 led to the suspension of Celtic art in the Scottish Highlands for a period. But it was not suppressed permanently, for it was in Scotland that the renewal of Celtic art began. Scottish national romanticism, promoted by Sir Walter Scott, was given a great boost by King George IV's visit to Edinburgh in 1822. Highland costume became respectable once more, seen as the true expression of Scottishness. New Celtic jewelry, based on surviving examples, became fashionable again.

The restored tradition was further reinforced by Queen Victoria, whose consort, Prince Albert, adopted Scottish modes of dress and designed a new royal tartan, called Balmoral. Under Queen Victoria, there was a general renewal of Christian art in the United Kingdom, which at that time included the whole of Ireland. Celtic art was recognized as

LEFT: *This depiction of King Arthur from the* Chronicle *of Peter Langtoft betrays a clear Norman influence; interest in Arthur as a historical figure has recently grown.*

the earliest Christian style of the British Isles, and especially relevant to Wales, Scotland, and Ireland. This renewed interest in Celtic art is often called "The Celtic Revival," but this is a false view, for it was not a revival of a dead art, but a conscious restoration of a living tradition.

Collections of Celtic artifacts, and archeological discoveries, published in the nineteenth century, assisted the new Celtic artists in their work. Romantic historical artists like Henry, Hornel, and Hole integrated Celtic artifacts from different places and periods into their historic paintings, expressing the essential spirit of the Celtic tradition. By the end of the nineteenth century, antiquaries and archeologists were making systematic studies of Celtic art. Among them are A. G. Langdon, who published *Old Cornish Crosses* in 1896, and J. Romilly Allen, who laid the foundations for the restoration of Celtic art. Romilly Allen's books, *The Early Christian Monuments of Scotland (1903) and Celtic Culture in Pagan* and *Pre-Christian Times* (1904), were the first to analyze Celtic art in a systematic way. Following his work was one of the most influential Celtic artists of the 20th century, George Bain. From the 1920s, he studied examples of Celtic art from Pictish stones and Celtic manuscripts, and developed principles based upon Romilly Allen's rediscoveries. Bain wanted to bring Celtic art back into the repertoire of contemporary artists, craftspeople, and designers, and succeeded. His work, *Celtic Art: The Methods of Construction*, first published in 1951, describes in detail most of the principles underlying Celtic art. It has become the stand-ard work on Celtic art, and remains the greatest influence on Celtic artists today. Because of the patient work of Romilly Allen, George Bain, and the Irish artist John G. Merne, the principles of Celtic art are available to all. Today, there is a vast repertoire of contem-porary Celtic art.

A charming medieval depiction of a boar. The Celts venerated boars both as symbols of hunting and war, but also of food and feasting.

ARTISTIC CONTINUITY

In the high medieval period, the style of Christian art misnamed "Gothic" reigned supreme. Over the years, Celtic crosses, formerly the height of Christian art, were progressively simplified, or replaced by more ornate high crosses in the medieval style. Celtic manuscripts, too, lost the intensity and intricacy of the *Book of Kells* and *Lindisfarne Gospels*. The monkish scribes, under Benedictine influence, developed a new style, and Celtic principles of layout and design were superseded. But although Celtic art was no longer employed by the church and royal courts, Celtic artistic traditions did not die out. They were maintained by secular craftspeople in Ireland, parts of Wales, the west Highlands of Scotland, and on the holy island of Iona. It was an ancestral heritage whose techniques and principles had been handed down from father to son and mother to daughter over many generations.

There still exist several late medieval artifacts that are recognizably traditional Celtic art. Preserved at Trinity College in Dublin is the fifteenth-century leather satchel made to protect the ancient *Book of Armagh*. It bears stamped Celtic ribbon-work and animal interlaces. Displayed in the National Museum of Antiquities in Edinburgh is the wonderful ivory and metal Eglinton Casket. It is one of the finest examples of sixteenth-century west Highland art. Another fine example of Celtic continuity there is a seventeenth-century brass ring brooch from Tomintoul, tooled with masterly knotwork roundels. The Celtic interlace patterns on these and other artifacts show that the craftspeople had a perfect knowledge and understanding of traditional Celtic art.

CULTURAL NATIONALISM

After the abolition of the Catholic Church in Britain, Catholic Gaelic Ireland was marginalized within its own land by an Anglican ruling class, who came largely, but not exclusively, from Great Britain. While English-speaking Ireland in the eighteenth century was associated with the worldwide Empire, that appeared to stand for progress in trade, science, and the arts, Irish-speaking Ireland seemed to be a backward and doomed

BOOK OF KELLS

This beautifully illustrated Celtic manuscript contains the four Gospels and was started at the monastery of Iona during the second half of the eighth century. It became known as The Book of Kells *because the monks fled the monastery to escape invading Norsemen and took refuge in the Abbey of Kells.*

relic of ancient barbarism. But then, as in the other Celtic lands, educated people in Ireland began to take a new interest in their indigenous history and culture. In 1753, Charles O'Conor called for an academy for the preservation of the Irish language, which was echoed by Sylvester O'Halloran in 1770. After that, ancient Irish manuscripts were rediscovered and published. Then a strange reversal took place, when students of Irish culture realized that their own tradi-tions were as ancient and valuable as those of their conquerors.

Indeed, Irish culture was seen as one of the formative elements of

European civilization. Charles O'Conor wrote that the Irish language was "the most original and unmixed now remaining in any part of Europe." The new-found pride in Irish traditions looked back to ancient pagan models for reforming the nation, and sought to write an authentic history of Ireland. O'Conor praised Ollamh Fodhla, traditional founder of the nation, who was both a wise philosopher and a good king. Ancient Irish sagas celebrated the ideals of a military aristocracy, where honor and loyalty were paramount, and the idea of "the life-spirit" of the Irish people was recognized. The ancient idea of Ireland as a holy island, independent of outside control, emerged from this new understanding of cultural identity.

From this culturo-political re-emergence, the Irish patriot movement of the 1760s led in 1782 to the Irish Parliament gaining the right

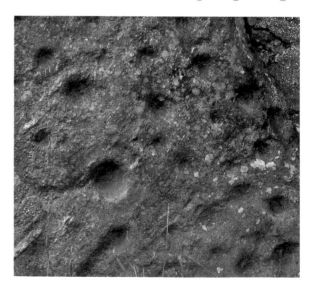

RIGHT: *Carved, circular, ring, and cup marks pit the surface of a stone at Brahan Castle, that is said to have legendary links with the Brahan Seer.*

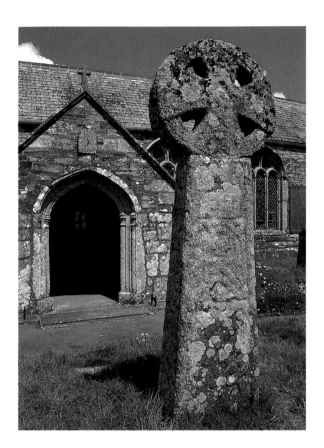

Potato Famine of 1846, calls for an independent Ireland became stronger, and direct action led to the foundation of armed groups dedicated to independence.

In 1916, an uprising was staged in Dublin, symbolically on Easter Sunday. It had little local support, and was put down by the United Kingdom army. But the subsequent execution of the survivors changed public opinion in Catholic Ireland. After a guerrilla war against the Union, a peace agreement was reached in which most of Ireland gained independence in 1922 as the Irish Free State. Six counties of Ulster remained in the United Kingdom. The success of Irish nationalism has led to the formation of nationalist and separatist movements in Brittany, Scotland, and Wales, whose supporters strive for independence for those lands from France and the United Kingdom.

LEFT: *An ancient Celtic wheel-cross stands proud in Cardinham churchyard in Cornwall, England. Such pierced, "four-hole" crosses are typical of Cornish style.*

to make its own laws. In 1791, the Society of United Irishmen was founded. In keeping with the Celtic spirit, symbolic acts were always part of the Irish nationalist repertoire. The United Irishmen staged an unsuccessful rebellion for an Irish Republic in 1798. After that, the Irish Parliament was dissolved, and Ireland was joined politically with Britain, in 1801, by an Act of Union. In 1803, Robert Emmett attempted to capture Dublin Castle and set up a republic. He failed, and was executed along with his followers. But by the middle of the nineteenth century, following the catastrophic

1916 EASTER UPRISING

Led by Patrick Pearce of the Irish Republican Brotherhood and James Connolly of Sinn Fein, an uprising against British rule in Ireland was staged in Dublin in 1916, symbolically on Easter Sunday, the Christian day of resurrection. However, the rebellion had little local support and was put down with armed force by the United Kingdom army.

CHAPTER 10

THE CELTIC SPIRIT
AT THE MILLENNIUM

THE HISTORY OF THE CELTS is long and illustrious by any criteria and primarily it can be seen in terms of the maintenance of human dignity in adversity. Time and again, Celtic nations have suffered defeat, but the tenacious spirit of Celtic culture has supported the people through every time of enormous difficulty. The Celts have been sustained by their traditional spiritual values, expressed through both pagan and Christian interpretations. The resistance of the Druids to Roman rule, the fortitude of the Celtic saints, the inspiration of the medieval Bards, and since the eighteenth century, the restoration of Celtic paganism by the modern Druids and others have all helped to retain this recognition and celebration of the divine in the material world.

SPIRITUAL CHAOS

The twentieth century has been a time of almost continuous technological warfare fought with an ideological ferocity scarcely seen since the time of Genghis Khan. These wars have brought a serious disruption of traditional ways of life and thought. Most importantly, they have brought a crisis of faith in the trustworthiness of both human and divine powers. With technological progress has come spiritual chaos and the destruction of the environment. This is a time of turmoil on a par with the age of the Celtic saints, who, during times of social and spiritual breakdown, were faithful to the principles and brought a measure of spiritual stability to an age of chaos.

CONTEMPORARY CELTS

Celtic spirituality is timeless and not just the legacy of a bygone age. It has never died out because the essence of Celtic wisdom is rooted in the deepest eternal secrets of existence. More and more people are realizing that the old traditions of the Druids, Bards, and Celtic saints are not useless remains of ignorance and superstition, but contain a valuable awareness of our harmony with nature. The sayings and prayers of the Celtic saints are easily available in many languages, while their holy places are visited by increasing numbers of pilgrims. Druidic philosophy is also a living and developing tradition, bringing valuable spiritual insights to contemporary society. Celtic culture, and especially Celtic spirituality, one of the oldest traditions of Europe, still has a lot to offer in the new millennium.

Silbury Hill in Avebury, Wiltshire, England is, according to legend, the burial place of King Sil and his golden horse.